A Passion for Food
The Superquinn Cookbook

Published in Ireland in 2010 by Harmonia
on behalf of Superquinn

© Superquinn 2010

Harmonia Ltd.
Rosemount House, Dundrum Road, Dublin 14
Tel: +353 (0)1 240 5300
Fax: +353 (0)1 661 9757
email: info@harmonia.ie
web: www.harmonia.ie

First printing

ISBN Number 978-0-9548576-4-6

WRITTEN BY Orla Broderick

DESIGN AND PRODUCTION David Gibbons

PHOTOGRAPHY Harry Weir

FOOD STYLIST Sharon Hearne-Smith

Acknowledgments

With many thanks to all of our Superquinn customers and colleagues,
without whom this book would not have been possible.

A huge thank you to Senator Feargal Quinn for his delicious mussels
recipe and the entertaining foreword to this book.

Special thanks to our wonderful contributing chefs, Ross Lewis,
Neven Maguire, Declan Furlong from Barretstown, and Donal Skehan.

Many thanks to Bord Bia for their invaluable support throughout
the project.

A special thank you to Orla Broderick, David Gibbons,
Sharon Herne-Smith and Harry Weir for working tirelessly
and always with a smile.

Well done and thank you to all of our winning customers and
colleagues for their mouth watering recipes.

Many thanks to all the team at Harmonia Publishing.

Finally, thanks to the team at Superquinn for making this happen:
Alison Hunter, Bruce Langlands, Richard Moriarty and Fiona Sweeney

A passion for FOOD

THE SUPERQUINN COOK BOOK

CONTENTS

THE RECIPES

A WORD WITH — SENATOR FEARGAL QUINN,
FOUNDER & NON EXECUTIVE PRESIDENT
OF SUPERQUINN

talking SHOP

Feargal Quinn opened his first shop, Quinn's, in Dundalk in 1960, when he was just 23 years old, marking the birth of an iconic Irish retail brand. Fifty years on and Superquinn has a nationwide chain of 23 stores employing more than 3,000 people, while the name Superquinn is synonymous with great food quality and excellent customer service.

"The Superquinn story all started for me," begins Feargal, "with a trip to France in my early twenties. I went off to France when I graduated from university to learn the trade there. But when I got home all I could talk about was this radical notion of 'self-service' that I had experienced in the shops in France. I was bursting to tell my father about the shoe shops where rows of left-foot shoes were laid out for customers to try, as opposed to the closed boxes behind the counter that we had in Ireland."

The passion for serving the customer was clearly apparent in Superquinn from the very beginning. "The notion of the customer selecting their own products was truly revolutionary at the time", recalls Feargal, "the idea of shopping with a basket threw them. I remember offering ladies baskets and they would decline so I would politely insist – and then they would end up taking them home with them!"

"We were always looking for ways to give our customers more and keep our staff inspired so we started sending our butchers on cookery courses so that they could advise the customers on how best to prepare any given cut of meat. We were the leaders in Ireland to employ expert butchers and bakers to work in-store."

The other great passion at Superquinn is of course food; providing Ireland with top quality, fresh food. In 1973 the company pioneered the idea of in-store food manufacturing developing a whole range of specialist fresh food departments

including the delicatessen, pizza kitchen, salad kitchen and scratch bakery where their signature fresh bread is baked daily from 5am. Another signature product for Superquinn which undoubtedly gives them an edge is the famous Superquinn sausage!

"The story behind the sausage dates back to the 70's when I got a call inviting me on a visit to a famous supermarket in Nuremburg, Germany. This supermarket was located beside a sausage factory and inside there was only a glass wall dividing the two; so you could watch your sausages being made before ordering them. Needless to say these were some of the best sausages I ever tasted. So I came home bursting to do the same. We embarked on an exhaustive

series of trials and tests to come up with the best sausage recipe and our tasty Superquinn sausage has been winning awards ever since."

"For me, Superquinn has always been about delivering the best – the best quality food, prepared and served by the best staff at the best price. At Superquinn the customer is king and I think this is all to the good for the future of Irish food."

Talking to Feargal his passion for food is clear and he takes great pride in the contribution Superquinn has made to Irish dinner tables over the past fifty years. This cookbook is a celebration of both past successes and future achievements.

Enjoy.

WINE
tips & tricks

"Some lighter red wines (Beaujolais, Valpolicella) do benefit from half an hour in the fridge before you open them up."

Storing Wine

These days wine is generally purchased with the weekly shop and consumed over the course of the week, therefore you don't really need to concern yourself too much with storing wine. However, if you are looking at buying a few cases of wine to keep for more than a week there are a few tips and tricks that can help you to get the most out of your collection.

A wine cellar is the most ideal way of keeping wine, but is restricted to people lucky to have the space. The next best option, also for serious wine enthusiasts, is to buy a wine storage cabinet that keeps your reds and whites at the perfect temperature and humidity. For most of us though, the wine cellar is a rack somewhere in the house, so here are the basic rules to follow:

Ensure that all bottles are left lying horizontally to ensure the cork is kept moist which stops it shrinking and letting in air. This is less important for screwcap wines but still recommended.

Keep your wines away from areas where there are great fluctuations in temperature and also anywhere that is too cold or too hot. Make sure that the bottles are out of direct sunlight as this can have a serious detrimental effect on wine. Keep your wines in an area that is also free from strong odours.

Serving Wine

Temperature

There are two general rules when it comes to serving wine and that is that red wine should be served at room temperature and white wines should be served chilled. This is certainly true, but some lighter red wines (Beaujolais, Valpolicella) do benefit from half an hour in the fridge before you open them up. In terms of rosé wines and champagnes, treat them the same as you would a white wine, which is around two hours in the fridge before opening. If you are in a hurry then you can always pop a bottle in the freezer for quick chilling but be careful not to let it freeze!

Opening a bottle

These days screw cap wines are becoming more popular but there are still plenty of wines out there still using corks. There are many different corkscrews on the market so my advice would be to try a few and stick to one that you like.

When it comes to champagne, firstly make sure that it is chilled as the colder the liquid the less pressure there is in the bottle. Then remove the wire closure, holding bottle away from you and in a safe direction. Finally, hold the cork firmly with one hand, using the other hand to twist the bottle and the cork should just glide out under its own pressure.

Letting a wine breathe

Generally, only red wines benefit from being 'left to breathe' especially full bodied reds such as Bordeaux or Shiraz. Most people let a wine breathe by opening the bottle an hour before drinking it and leaving it on the sideboard, but this actually has little or no effect as the amount of wine in contact with the air is about the size of a 10c piece. To allow a wine to "breathe" you should pour the contents of the bottle into a good sized decanter to allow the wine to move about and react with oxygen.

Decanting

As well as the most effective way to allow a wine breathe, decanters are also used for red wines that have a sediment. Sediment comes from age and is the effect of the anthocyanins (the colour component of wine) very slowly coming out of solution in the wine and falling to the bottom of the bottle along with a few other components such as proteins and tartrates. This sediment is entirely harmless but it is unsightly and can be bitter and so you are best not to have it in your glass. If you suspect that a red wine has a sediment then decanting it is easy as long as you follow these steps:

In the days or even weeks before you drink the wine carefully move the bottle from your rack into an upright position to allow the sediment to fall to the bottom of the bottle.

On the day you want to drink the wine open the bottle in the normal way, carefully avoiding shaking it too much. Place a light behind the decanter and the bottle so that you can see through the neck of the bottle of wine.

Carefully begin to pour the wine into the decanter watching the wine though the neck of the bottle, looking out for any sediment.

It's fine to allow some sediment into the decanter, but when the flow of sediment becomes to strong, stop pouring. (If you are unsure it is fine to place a piece of muslin or gauze over the neck of the decanter to catch any sediment.)

What is a corked wine?

There are many 'faults' that can occur in wine, but cork taint is one of the most common and recognisable. You can tell a corked wine usually by smelling it (this is the reason why a sommelier in a restaurant offers you a small sample of the wine before they pour a full glass). The smell of a corked wine has been described in many ways but some usual ways are moldy newspaper, wet dog, damp cloth, or a damp, musty cellar. This smell is a chemical called TCA and is the result of a naturally occurring fungus that is present all around us getting into the cork and reacting with oxygen and the wine to give off this foul smelling chemical. The only real way of preventing this cork taint is not to use corks, which is why producers are turning to synthetic corks and screwcaps more and more.

Glasses

The main thing to remember with wine glasses is to only fill them half way to allow the drinker to swirl the wine in the glass and to allow more aroma's to come through. A tulip shaped glass that tapers towards the top will also allow you to swirl the wine around with less risk of making a mess. In general a standard wine bottle should serve six glasses of wine. In terms of champagne, avoid at all costs the wide flat 'bowls' that were popular a few years ago, but instead use tall, thin flutes as these will retain the fizz far longer and again helps to avoid spills. Also when it comes to champagne avoid washing glasses with detergent as the very chemicals in the detergent that makes them cut through grime, also destroy the champagne bubbles. If you can't avoid using detergent rinse your glasses out with water and dry them very well.

Wine and food

There are plenty of so called 'rules' around what wine to drink with which food, but in general the most important thing is that you choose a wine that you enjoy. There is no use buying a red wine to go with steak if you never drink red wine! There are however, some general guidelines that do work to help you to create the perfect match for your meal:

- ► It's an old adage that red wine goes with red meat and white wine with white meat and fish, but this is generally true.

- ► If your dish is quite oily (fish) or fatty (lamb/duck) try a wine with natural high acidity to cut through the oil and fat. Try a dry Riesling with fish or a Pinot Noir with duck.

- ► Think about the sauce that you are serving with the meal as well as the main ingredient. For example, try a Red Burgundy as a match with turkey for its luscious redcurrants and cranberry fruit flavours. With creamy dishes, try a creamy Chardonnay.

- ► Dry rosé wines are a great match with spicy foods as are the white wines from the Alsace region of France.

- ► If you are using a wine in a recipe, then serve the same wine with the meal. It ties in beautifully.

- ► If you are having a big occasion and you are keen to impress, try the wine before hand to make sure that you like it.

- ► A different wine with different courses works really well and don't forget the dessert wine as a great way to round off a meal.

Recipe wine matches

To help you complete a simple meal for two or the perfect dinner party menu, we have offered you some suggestions of the wines that we feel best compliment the recipes in this book. Remember it is important that you always buy what you like and where possible try before you buy. Drop into your local Superquinn store where the trained wine experts will be happy to offer you advice and recommendations.

WEIGH
the difference

Weights and Measurements

The aim of this book is to make cooking as straightforward and pleasurable as it can be. The clear instructions should help get you impressive results. However there are a number of general guidelines, which you should follow in order to get the best out of the recipes.

▶ Both metric and imperial measurements are given for the recipes with the exception of when a full packet or can has been used. Follow either metric or imperial throughout, as they are not interchangeable. Use the following reference charts if you need to convert or adapt any measurements yourself.

▶ Make sure you read the line on the measuring jug at eye level when measuring liquids.

▶ All spoon measurements are level unless otherwise stated. Sets of measuring spoons are readily available for accurate measurements of small quantities. Do not hold the measuring spoon into which you are pouring the liquid over the dish you are making, in case you pour out too much.

▶ Ovens should be preheated to the specified temperature, as should grills. The cooking times in the recipes assume that this has already been done.

▶ Large eggs should be used except where otherwise specified.

Conversion tables

Conversions are approximate and have been rounded up or down. Follow one set of measurements only – do not mix metric and Imperial.

Weights

Metric	Imperial
15 g	½ oz
25 g	1 oz
40 g	1½ oz
50 g	2 oz
75 g	3 oz
100 g	4 oz
150 g	5 oz
175 g	6 oz
200 g	7 oz
225 g	8 oz
250 g	9 oz
275 g	10 oz
350 g	12 oz
375 g	13 oz
400 g	14 oz
425 g	15 oz
450 g	1 lb
550 g	1¼ lb
675 g	1½ lb
900 g	2 lb
1.5 kg	3 lb
1.75 kg	4 lb
2.25 kg	5 lb

Volume

Metric	Imperial
25 ml	1 fl oz
50 ml	2 fl oz
85 ml	3 fl oz
150 ml	¼ pint
300 ml	½ pint
450 ml	¾ pint
600 ml	1 pint
700 ml	1¼ pints
900 ml	1½ pints
1 litre	1¾ pints
1.2 litres	2 pints
1.25 litres	2¼ pints
1.5 litres	2½ pints
1.6 litres	2¾ pints
1.75 litres	3 pints
1.8 litres	3¼ pints
2 litres	3½ pints
2.1 litres	3¾ pints
2.25 litres	4 pints
2.75 litres	5 pints
3.4 litres	6 pints
3.9 litres	7 pints
5 litres	8 pints

Measurements

Metric	Imperial
5 mm	¼ inch
1 cm	½ inch
2.5 cm	1 inch
5 cm	2 inches
7.5 cm	3 inches
10 cm	4 inches
15 cm	6 inches
18 cm	7 inches
20 cm	8 inches
23 cm	9 inches
25 cm	10 inches
30 cm	12 inches

Oven temperatures

140°C	275°F	Gas mark 1
150°C	300°F	Gas mark 2
160°C	325°F	Gas mark 3
180°C	350°F	Gas mark 4
190°C	375°F	Gas mark 5
200°C	400°F	Gas mark 6
220°C	425°F	Gas mark 7
230°C	450°F	Gas mark 8
240°C	475°F	Gas mark 9

store cupboard
ESSENTIALS

Shopping checklist

Many of the ingredients used in this book can be found in a well-stocked store cupboard. It may seem like a long list but if you're an enthusiastic cook you'll be amazed at how much you already have. When you haven't got too much to buy in your weekly shop throw a couple of 'treats' into your trolley to save for a rainy day. Most things have quite a good shelf life, while others, once opened should be kept in the fridge.

However, there is no point in having cramped cupboards,if you don't know what you have or where anything is, and when you do finally manage to pull something out it's well past its sell-by-date. So be sensible and make the most of the space available to you, making sure it's well ventilated and that there is a regular turnover of ingredients. Remember, this list is only a guide and needs to be tailored to suit your own requirements.

Canned foods

- ▶ Chopped tomatoes
- ▶ White beans such as chickpeas or cannellini beans
- ▶ Coconut milk
- ▶ Tuna
- ▶ Anchovies
- ▶ Black olives
- ▶ Condensed milk

Bottle and jars

- ▶ Sunflower oil
- ▶ Olive and extra virgin olive oil
- ▶ Toasted sesame oil
- ▶ Duck/goose fat
- ▶ White wine and red wine vinegar
- ▶ Balsamic vinegar
- ▶ Soy sauce
- ▶ Tomato ketchup
- ▶ Wholegrain, Dijon mustard and prepared English mustard
- ▶ Worcestershire sauce
- ▶ Thai fish sauce (nam pla)
- ▶ Creamed horseradish
- ▶ Redcurrant jelly
- ▶ Capers
- ▶ Mayonnaise
- ▶ Clear honey
- ▶ Golden syrup
- ▶ Black treacle
- ▶ Vanilla extract
- ▶ Red and white wine
- ▶ Sun-dried tomatoes
- ▶ Roasted red peppers
- ▶ Artichoke hearts
- ▶ Red onion marmalade

Dried goods

- ▶ Baking powder
- ▶ Bicarbonate of soda
- ▶ Bread soda
- ▶ Plain flour, strong white and self-raising
- ▶ Fast action dried yeast
- ▶ Spaghetti
- ▶ Risotto and pudding rice
- ▶ Semolina
- ▶ Plain chocolate
- ▶ Golden caster sugar, light muscovado and icing sugar
- ▶ Stock cubes
- ▶ Maldon sea salt
- ▶ Herbs and spices: black peppercorns, ground cumin, coriander, paprika, cloves, ginger, cinnamon, cayenne, chilli powder, Cajun seasoning and vanilla pods
- ▶ Dried fruit such as raisins, figs and prunes
- ▶ Nuts such as walnuts, pine nuts and hazelnuts
- ▶ Sesame seeds

In the fridge

It is a good idea to always have the following essentials. Many have long sell-by-dates and will keep well if stored in the right conditions. If possible, take cheese out of the fridge at least 30 minutes before use. Use fresh wrapping for further storage. Eggs absorb other smells easily so they need to be kept away from any strong smelling foods. Keep them with the pointed end downwards and bring back to room temperature before use.

- ▶ Milk
- ▶ Buttermilk
- ▶ Eggs
- ▶ Butter
- ▶ Cream, soured cream, crème fraîche, Greek style and natural yoghurt
- ▶ Mascarpone cheese
- ▶ Chilled custard
- ▶ Parmesan
- ▶ Vintage Cheddar
- ▶ Smoked or plain streaky bacon rashers
- ▶ Parma ham

Groceries

Keep citrus fruits in the salad compartment at the bottom of your fridge, along with the other vegetables. Chillies, spring onions and ginger all benefit from being stored in airtight plastic bags.

- Spring onions
- Tomatoes
- Garlic
- Onions and shallots
- Red chillies
- Ginger
- Potatoes
- Celery
- Carrots
- Oranges, lemons and limes
- Soft flour tortillas
- Loaf of bread

In the freezer

- Garden peas
- Vanilla ice cream
- Puff and filo pastry
- Breadcrumbs

On the windowsill

Use fresh herbs for their powerful and pungent flavours and it is now very easy to have a good selection of growing herbs on the windowsill. Not only do they look attractive but they are excellent value for money.

Parsley and chives are essential, while basil, thyme, sage, bay leaves, coriander, mint, tarragon, rosemary, dill and chervil are all useful additions. They just need to be watered occasionally to thrive, and picking the new shoots encourages the rest of the plant to fill out.

Essential equipment

Be kind to yourself when buying your kitchen essentials. Good quality equipment will last for years and actually improve your cooking.

- 1 large sharp knife
- 1 small sharp knife
- 1 carving knife
- 1 chef's steel/knife sharpener
- Can opener
- Chopping board
- Large non-stick frying pan
- 3 sizes of saucepans (small, medium and large)
- 3 wooden spoons
- Kitchen scales
- Set of mixing bowls
- Colander
- Measuring jug
- Metal hand whisk
- Sieve (get a decent size)
- Slotted spoon
- Fish slice
- Potato masher
- Vegetable peeler
- Box grater
- Pastry brush
- Rolling pin
- Roasting tin
- Baking sheet

Useful extra equipment

The following items are not essential but will make your life a lot easier and enable you to become a more accomplished cook.

- Tongs
- Palette knife
- Hand blender
- Electric mixer
- Food processor
- Wok
- Lemon juicer
- Flour dredger
- Set of ramekins (standard size)
- Casserole dish with lid (preferably ceramic)
- Cast-iron griddle pan (with metal handle)
- Fluted cutter (box set)
- Mandolin
- Muffin tin

THE BAKERY
thorough BREAD

THE BAKERY

I s there anything more intoxicating than the smell of freshly baked bread, wafting warm and heavy on the air? Nothing beats it – and that's why Superquinn were the first, and continue to be the only, supermarket to boast in-store bakeries, making freshly baked goods from scratch every day from 5am.

Bread never tastes better than when it's still warm. Who can resist blueberry soda bread straight from the oven or the salty, olive oil-infused flavour of foccaccia stuffed with mozzarella, pesto and roasted peppers? Can there be anything better than the tangy, malty finish of sourdough or the nutty, wholesome texture of a multi-seed brown loaf served with smoked salmon and lemon for a luxuriously simple lunch.

Forget fussy dinner parties - if you want to impress and delight your friends, just whip a batch of chocolate scones from the oven when they pop by for tea. Serve them cut open and spread with whipped cream for instant afternoon tea heaven.

slice of HEAVEN

These pizza toasts are much better than any ready-made versions and actually quite simple to make. The dough needs very little kneading time and doesn't even need time to rise, making the bases easier to roll out.

Garlic bread pizza toasts

Makes 8

550 g (1 ¼ lb) strong white flour, plus extra for dusting

7 g sachet fast action dried yeast

4 tbsp olive oil, plus a little extra

2 large garlic cloves, finely chopped

350 g (12 oz) small vine-ripened tomatoes cut into quarters

one good handful fresh basil leaves

3 tbsp extra virgin olive oil

1 tsp balsamic vinegar

Maldon sea salt and freshly ground black pepper

To download the shopping list:
www.superquinn.ie/content/GarlicBread PizzaToasts/899

Wine match
Valpolicella
The perfect match for this simple pizza is a modest light red wine that reinforces the Italian character.

1 Preheat the oven to 230°C (450°F), Gas mark 8. Mix the flour in a bowl with the yeast and one teaspoon of salt. Make a well in the centre and pour in two tablespoons of the olive oil and 300 ml (½ pint) of warm water and stir vigorously until the mixture comes together.

2 Turn out on to a lightly floured surface and knead until the mixture forms a ball. Cut into eight pieces. Take one piece, leaving the rest covered loosely with oiled cling film. Lightly flour the work surface again and roll the dough out to an oval shape about 15 cm (6 in) in diameter. Place on a baking sheet. Mix the rest of the olive oil with the garlic and drizzle a little on top. Repeat with the remaining pieces of dough and bake for 12-14 minutes until the pizza bases are crisp and cooked through. You should be able to fit four pizza bases on each baking sheet so will have to use two baking sheets.

3 Meanwhile, place the tomatoes in a bowl and tear in the basil leaves. Dress with the extra virgin olive oil and balsamic vinegar, then season to taste. As soon as the pizza bases come out of the oven, spoon over some of the tomato mixture and serve immediately on warmed plates.

Chef's top tip —

If you don't want to go to the trouble of making your own pizza bases try using white pitta breads instead. Drizzle on the garlic oil and flash through the oven for 2-3 minutes before adding the tomato and basil topping.

upperCRUST

> This bread can also be flavoured with a tablespoon of chopped fresh herbs, such as thyme or rosemary for a more pronounced taste or add 4 tablespoons of chopped fresh mixed herbs, such as flat-leaf parsley, basil and chives.

Rustic Mediterranean bread

Makes 1 large loaf

675 g (1½ lb) strong white flour, plus extra for dusting

2 x 7 g sachets fast action dried yeast, about 1 tbsp in total

100 g (4 oz) sun-dried tomato bruschetta topping (from a jar)

2 tsp fennel seeds

1 tsp Maldon salt

olive oil, for greasing

To download the shopping list:
www.superquinn.ie/content/
RusticMediterraneanBread/900

Wine match
Côtes du Rhône
This dish is best complimented by the fruitiness of the Côtes du Rhône.

Chef's top tip –
A handful of diced sun-dried tomatoes that have been preserved in oil also works well if you haven't got the sun-dried tomato bruschetta topping.

1 Place the flour in the bowl of a food mixer fitted with a dough attachment if you have one. Add the yeast, two tablespoons of sun-dried tomato bruschetta topping, fennel seeds and 500 ml (18 fl oz) of warm water and the salt. Switch on the machine and mix until you have a very sloppy dough mixture. You can also do this by hand and mix with your fingers for 2–3 minutes, then knead to incorporate the flour, scraping the sides of the bowl and folding the dough over itself until it gathers into a rough mass.

2 Turn the dough out on to a well-floured surface and spread over the remainder of the sun-dried tomato bruschetta topping. Lightly flour your hands and knead in the sun-dried tomato bruschetta topping for 6–8 minutes until the dough is smooth and pliable. The dough will be very sticky at first; keep your hands and the work surface lightly floured, using a dough scraper if necessary to prevent it from sticking and building up on the work surface. As you continue kneading, the dough will become more elastic and easier to handle. Shape into a loose ball, then return it to a clean bowl and cover with cling film. Leave to rest for 20 minutes.

3 Turn the dough out again on to a well-floured surface and knead for 2–3 minutes or until it becomes springy and very smooth. Shape into a loose ball and place it in a lightly oiled large bowl. Turn to coat the dough with the oil and cover tightly with cling film. Leave to rise at room temperature for 1 hour, or until it looks slightly puffy but has not doubled in size.

4 Preheat the oven to 180°C (350°F), Gas mark 4. Remove the dough from the bowl and form it into a round shaped loaf. Bake for 45 minutes until the loaf is a deep golden brown and sounds hollow when tapped on the bottom. Transfer to a wire rack and leave to cool before cutting into slices to serve.

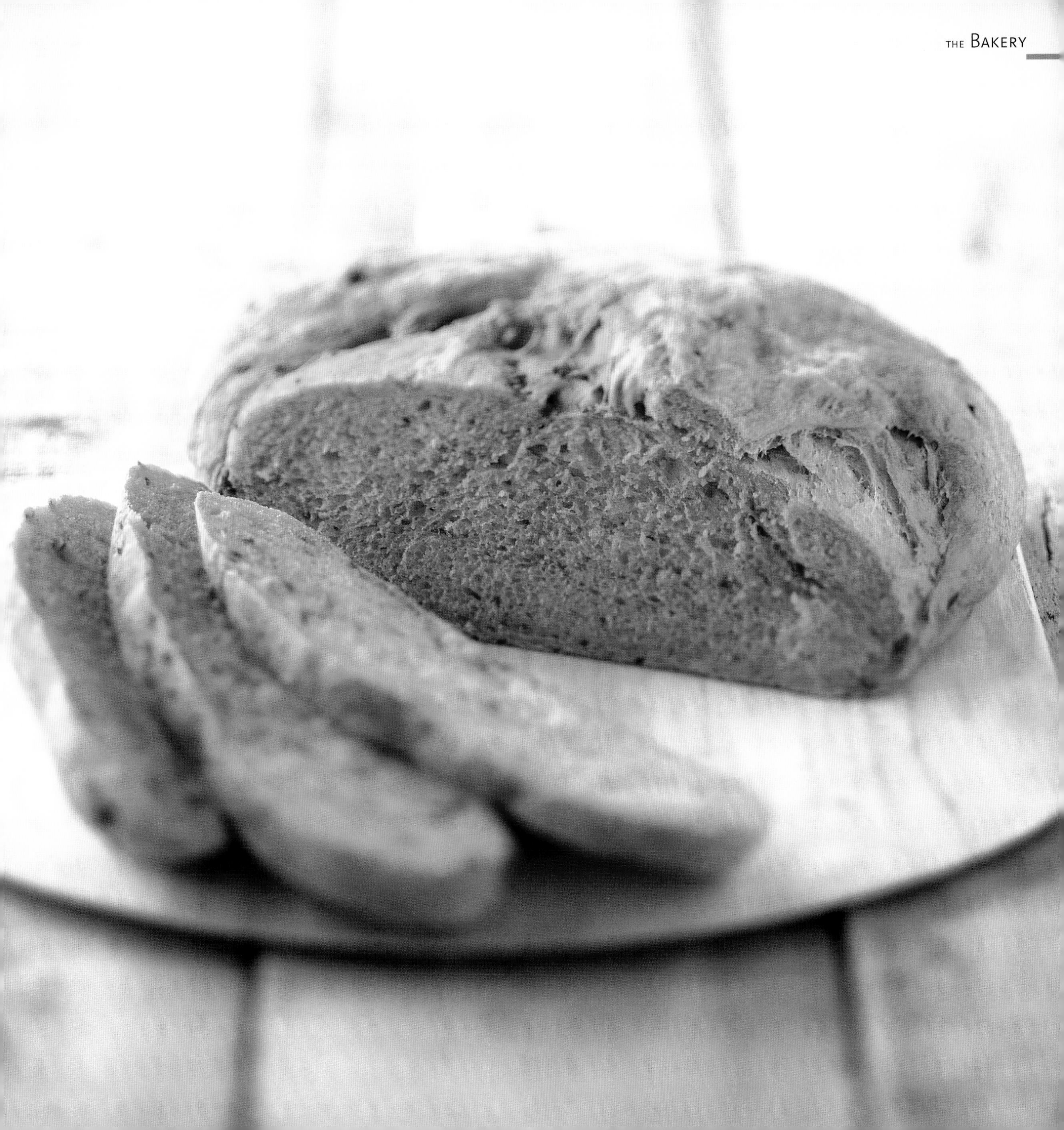

DOUGH delightful

This bread takes a little bit of preparation and time but the results are well worth the effort. Once the starter dough is made, leave it to stand for a few days to attract wild yeasts before adding to the bread dough. This bread has a slightly sour flavour and keeps for up to 3 days, wrapped in foil.

Sourdough bread

Makes 1 large loaf

675 g (1 ½ lb) strong white flour, plus extra for dusting

225 g (8 oz) wholegrain spelt flour

7 g sachet fast action dried yeast

1 tbsp caster sugar

1 tbsp Maldon sea salt

olive oil, for greasing

For the starter dough:

7 g sachet fast action dried yeast

225 g (8 oz) strong white flour

To download the shopping list:
www.superquinn.ie/content/Sourdough Bread/901

1 Make the sourdough starter three days in advance. Mix the yeast with a little warm water in a bowl. Stir in 600 ml (1 pint) of warm water with the white flour until smooth. Cover with a damp tea towel and leave in a warm, dark place for 3 days, stirring and spraying with a little water from time to time.

2 To make the bread, place the white flour, spelt flour and yeast in a bowl with the sugar and salt. Gradually work in 120 ml (4 fl oz) of the starter dough and enough warm water to form a soft dough. You will need between 375 ml and 450 ml (13 fl oz and ¾ pint) of water depending on the type of flours you use. Knead on a lightly floured surface for 10 minutes until soft and pliable.

3 Shape the dough into a ball and place in a large oiled bowl. Cover with oiled cling film and leave it to rise in a warm place for 1 ½ hours or until doubled in size.

4 Knock back the dough on a lightly floured surface and shape into a flattish round. Carefully score the surface in a diamond pattern. Place on a floured baking sheet, cover with oiled cling film and leave it to rise for another 30 minutes.

5 Preheat the oven to 230°C (450°F), Gas mark 8 for 15 minutes, then lower the temperature to 190°C (375°F), Gas mark 5 and bake for another 20–25 minutes until the bread sounds hollow when tapped underneath. Transfer to wire rack to cool, then cut into slices to serve.

berry GOOD

This soda bread is just delicious served warm and should be eaten quickly. However, it can be frozen on the day you bake it. If you are not planning to eat it for a few hours, sprinkle the loaf with a little water and wrap in a clean tea towel to prevent the crust becoming too hard.

Blueberry soda bread

Makes 1 loaf

450 g (1 lb) self-raising flour, plus extra for dusting

1 tsp salt

50 g (2 oz) butter, plus extra to serve

2 tsp caster sugar

125 g punnet blueberries

300 ml (½ pint) buttermilk, plus a little extra if necessary

 **To download the shopping list:**
www.superquinn.ie/content/Blueberry SodaBread/888

1 Preheat the oven to 220°C (425°F), Gas mark 7. Sift the flour and salt into a bowl. Rub in the butter with your fingertips until the mixture resembles fine breadcrumbs. Stir in the sugar and blueberries.

2 Pour all of the buttermilk into the blueberry mixture. With a spoon, gently and quickly stir into the flour until you have achieved a soft but not sticky dough, adding a little more buttermilk if necessary. Lightly flour the work surface.

3 Turn out the dough on a lightly floured surface and pat into a round that is about 3 cm (1 ½ in) thick. Transfer to a floured baking sheet and cut a deep cross with a sharp knife. Bake for 15 minutes.

4 Lower the temperature to 200°C (400°F), Gas mark 6 and bake for another 20 minutes or so until the bread sounds hollow when tapped on the bottom. Transfer to a wire rack and leave to cool for 15 minutes, then cut into slices and spread with butter to serve.

Chef's top tip –

To make this soda bread into scones simply cut the dough into 10 large triangles with a sharp knife. Bake for just 15 minutes.

EGGING you on

This has to be the ultimate bacon sandwich!
It's a good idea to cook the bases so that
you can start assembling the sandwiches
whilst the tops are cooking.

Eggy bread BLT

Serves 4

4 eggs

2 tbsp milk

1 large white pan (not sliced)

4 tbsp olive oil

**16 smoked streaky bacon rashers,
rinds removed**

1 tbsp Dijon mustard

**4 small vine-ripened tomatoes,
thinly sliced**

**25 g (1 oz) frisby lettuce
and / or rocket leaves**

2 tbsp mayonnaise

**Maldon sea salt and freshly
ground black pepper**

To download the shopping list:
www.superquinn.ie/content/EggyBread
BLT/902

1 Crack the eggs into a shallow dish, add the milk, season
generously and beat well with a fork to combine. Cut the pan
into eight thick slices, discarding the ends. Soak each slice of the
bread in the egg mixture, turning to coat.

2 Heat a large frying pan and add a thin film of the olive
oil, then add two slices of the soaked eggy bread. Cook over a
medium to low heat for about 1-2 minutes on each side until
golden brown. Keep warm while you cook the remainder.

3 Meanwhile, preheat the grill. Arrange the bacon on a grill
rack and cook for a couple of minutes on each side until really
crispy. Keep warm.

4 Just before serving, spread the Dijon mustard over the bases,
next add a layer of tomato slices and season generously. Top with
the bacon and then the lettuce and/or rocket leaves. Finish by
spreading the mayonnaise on the top halves of the eggy bread
and use to cover the sandwich fillings. Cut each eggy bread BLT
and arrange on plates to serve.

Chef's top tip –

*Make sure that your heat is not too high, otherwise
the bread may catch and brown too quickly.*

CUSTOMER RECIPE — HILARY O'CONNELL,
SUPERQUINN CARLOW

step GINGERLY

Gingerbread muffins

"My mother taught me how to make this quick and easy gingerbread. Of course you can double the recipe and bake it in a 900g (2 lb) lightly greased loaf tin at 180°C (350°F), Gas mark 4 for about an hour until just firm and a skewer inserted into the centre comes out clean."

Makes 9

1 small egg

4 tbsp black treacle

50 g (2 oz) light muscovado sugar

50 g (2 oz) butter

175 g (6 oz) plain flour

pinch of salt

½ tsp ground ginger

½ tsp ground cinnamon

½ tsp bread soda

To download the shopping list:
www.superquinn.ie/content/GingerBread
Muffins/903

1 Preheat the oven to 190°C (375°F), Gas mark 5. Place the egg, treacle and sugar in a large bowl and beat well to combine. Melt the butter in the microwave or in a small pan and beat in five tablespoons of hot water. In a separate bowl, sift the flour, salt, ginger, cinnamon and bread soda.

2 Beat the butter mixture into the egg, treacle and sugar and then beat in the flour mixture until just blended. Do not over mix. Divide the batter among a 9-hole muffin tin lined with paper cakes and bake for 15–20 minutes until risen and just beginning to crack in the middle. Leave to cool completely on a wire rack before arranging on plates to serve.

HILARY has shopped at Superquinn Carlow since it opened in 1994. She loves the service and appreciates how much the staff go out of their way to help customers.

STAFF RECIPE — GEORGINA DALY,
SUPERQUINN HEAD OFFICE

BEAN naughty

Espresso cupcakes

"Melt-in-the mouth cupcakes with a delicious creamy white chocolate topping, perfect for taking to someone's house for coffee."

Makes 12

1 tbsp espresso instant coffee

125 g (4 ½ oz) butter

125 g (4 ½ oz) caster sugar

125 g (4 ½ oz) self-raising flour

1 tsp baking powder

2 eggs, beaten

1– 2 tbsp milk

For the topping:

75 g (3 oz) white chocolate, broken into squares

25 g (1 oz) butter

50 g (2 oz) soured cream

125 g (4 ½ oz) icing sugar, sifted

25 g (1 oz) plain chocolate, finely grated

To download the shopping list:
www.superquinn.ie/content/Espresso Cupcakes/904

1 Preheat the oven to 180°C (350°F), Gas mark 4. Place the coffee in a small bowl and stir in one teaspoon of hot water, then set aside to cool.

2 Cream the butter and sugar in a large bowl until light and fluffy. Sift the flour and baking powder into a separate bowl. Add the beaten eggs and flour mixture alternately to the butter mixture and then beat in the coffee liquid.

3 Finally, beat in enough of the milk to make a dropping consistency. Divide the cupcake mixture among a 12-hole muffin tin that has been lined with paper cases. Bake for 18–20 minutes until well-risen and golden brown. Transfer to a wire rack and leave to cool completely.

4 To make the topping, melt the chocolate and butter together in a microwave or set over a pan of simmering water. Leave to cool and then beat in the soured cream. Add the sifted icing sugar and beat until thick.

5 When the muffins are cold, spread a thick layer of the topping over each one and finish with some grated plain chocolate. Arrange on plates to serve.

GEORGINA has worked in Superquinn for the last 22 years and has worked in almost every area of the business.

bread
for
SUCCESS

People just can't seem to get enough of flavoured breads and this one is a real winner. Of course you can experiment with the fillings; ricotta cheese would work well instead of the mozzarella, as would provolone or taleggio.

Mozzarella, pesto and roasted pepper focaccia

Makes 1 large loaf

900 g (2 lb) strong white flour, plus extra for dusting

7 g sachet fast action dried yeast

5 tbsp olive oil, plus extra for drizzling

6 tbsp basil pesto

2 x 100 g balls mozzarella, roughly torn

3 roasted peppers, cut in half (from a jar and preserved in oil)

Maldon sea salt and freshly ground black pepper

To download the shopping list:
www.superquinn.ie/content/MozzarellaPesto
AndRoastedPepperFocaccia/905

Wine match
Italian Soave
The rustic charm of this bread needs a simple, everyday wine. Italian is the natural choice and the gentle tones of the Soave compliment the pesto perfectly.

1 Mix the flour and yeast in a bowl. Make a well in the centre and pour in 600 ml (1 pint) of warm water with the olive oil to achieve a soft dough. Turn out on to a floured surface and then lightly flour your hands. Knead for about 10 minutes until the dough is smooth and pliable. Lightly oil a large bowl and put in the dough, then lightly oil the top. Cover with cling film and set aside for 1 hour or until the dough has doubled in size.

2 Preheat the oven to 220°C (425°F), Gas mark 7. When the dough has doubled in size, remove the cling film and, with a clenched fist, punch it down. Remove from the bowl and place on an oiled work surface. Knead for a couple of minutes until smooth, then roll out to a large rectangle, about 5 mm (¼ in) thick. Spread over the pesto, leaving a border around the edges and then scatter the mozzarella on top.

3 Arrange the roasted peppers on top of the cheese and season with pepper. Carefully roll the dough up like a Swiss roll to enclose the filling completely, tucking the ends in and place on a well-oiled baking sheet with the join underneath. Cover with oiled cling film and leave to rise again for about 30 minutes.

4 Dimple the surface of the dough and scatter the top with salt. Bake for about 40 minutes or until cooked through and pale golden. Check its progress whilst it's cooking and if it looks like it is starting to burn, turn the oven down a little. Transfer to a wire rack and leave to cool, then cut into slices to serve.

DARK. magic

For urgent times when the cupboard is bare of buttermilk, these scones work just as well by souring ordinary milk. Simply mix with one and a half tablespoons of lemon juice.

Chocolate chip scones

Makes 8

225 g (8 oz) self-raising flour, plus extra for dusting

pinch of salt

1 tsp baking powder

40 g (1 ½ oz) butter, plus extra to serve (optional)

50 g (2 oz) plain chocolate, finely chopped

about 150 ml (¼ pint) buttermilk

beaten egg, to glaze

To download the shopping list:
www.superquinn.ie/content/Chocolate
ChipScones/906

1 Preheat the oven to 220°C (425°F), Gas mark 7. Sift the flour, salt and baking powder into a bowl. Rub in the butter until the mixture resembles fine breadcrumbs.

2 Fold in the chocolate and then stir in enough buttermilk to give a fairly soft, light dough. It is important to add all of the liquid at once. If you add the liquid a trickle at a time it slows the whole process down and means the dough will be handled too much.

3 On a lightly floured surface, lightly roll out the dough to a 2 cm (¾ in) thickness and cut into rounds with a 6 cm (2 ½ in) cutter.

4 Place on a non-stick baking sheet and brush the tops with the beaten egg. Bake for about 10 minutes until well risen and golden brown. Cool on a wire rack. Serve warm, split and spread with butter (if liked) on individual plates.

tray CHIC

These muffins are delicious with a bowl of soup or chilli con carne that has been garnished with a dollop of soured cream and a few fresh coriander leaves. Of course, you could use ordinary bacon instead of the pancetta or omit altogether for a vegetarian option.

Pancetta and chilli muffins

Makes 12

50 g (2 oz) butter

1 tbsp olive oil

100 g (4 oz) pancetta (smoked bacon lardons)

150 g (5 oz) self-raising flour

2 tsp caster sugar

1 tsp celery salt

2 tsp baking powder

½ tsp cracked black pepper

150 g (5 oz) semolina

2 eggs, lightly beaten

300 ml (½ pint) buttermilk

1 red chilli, seeded and finely chopped

2 tbsp chopped fresh mixed herbs (such as flat-leaf parsley, chives and basil)

To download the shopping list:
www.superquinn.ie/content/PancettaAnd
ChilliMuffins/907

1 Preheat the oven to 180°C (350°F), Gas mark 4. Melt the butter in a small pan or in the microwave and use one tablespoon to grease a 12-hole muffin tin. Set the remainder aside. Heat the oil in a frying pan and cook the pancetta cubes until sizzling and lightly golden. Drain well on kitchen paper.

2 Sift the flour, sugar, celery salt and baking powder into a bowl, then tip in the pepper and semolina, stirring to combine. Make a well in the centre of the dry ingredients and quickly stir in the eggs, buttermilk and remaining melted butter until you have achieved a smooth batter.

3 Fold the crispy pancetta into the muffin batter with the chilli and herbs until just combined. Spoon into the prepared muffin tin and bake for about 20 minutes or until the muffins are golden brown and a skewer comes out clean. Arrange on a plate and serve warm or cold.

Wine match
Chilean Rosé
This dry rosé wine compliments both the chilli and pancetta.

TOP
seed

This bread makes the best use of the gluten-free bread mixes that are now available. It has a very different texture to ordinary bread. It is enriched with olive oil, seeds and some black treacle.

Gluten-free multi seed bread

Makes 1 loaf

250 g (9 oz) tritamyl white bread mix

100 g (4 oz) tritamyl brown bread mix

1 tsp salt

50 g (2 oz) mixed seeds

1 tbsp black treacle

2 tbsp olive oil, plus extra for greasing

375 ml (13 fl oz) buttermilk

butter, for spreading

To download the shopping list:
www.superquinn.ie/content/GlutenFree
MultiSeedBread/908

1 Preheat the oven to 200°C (400°F), Gas mark 6. Sieve the bread mixes into a bowl with the salt. Stir in the seeds, reserving one tablespoon as a topping.

2 Place the treacle, olive oil and buttermilk in a jug and mix well to combine. Make a well in the centre of the dry ingredients and pour in the buttermilk mixture, stirring to a smooth batter.

3 Pour the batter into a lightly oiled 900 g (2 lb) loaf tin. Use a spoon dipped in cold water to smooth the top. Make a cut lengthwise along the top of the loaf and sprinkle over the reserved tablespoon of seeds. Lightly cover the tin with oiled cling film and place in a warm place for 30 minutes until the dough is fairly well risen.

4 Bake the bread for 35–40 minutes until golden brown and crusty on top. Leave the loaf in the tin for 5 minutes and then transfer to a wire rack and allow to cool completely. Cut into slices and spread with butter to serve.

THE GREENGROCER
GROWTH
industry

THE GREENGROCER

The great thing about cooking with really fresh fruit and vegetables is that you get maximum taste with minimum effort. With Superquinn's policy of supporting Irish farmers and only sourcing the freshest and best quality ingredients you are guaranteed produce that is bursting with flavour and goodness. With raw materials this good there is little more you need to do.

There is nothing more satisfying than letting the seasons dictate your choice and enjoying the lightness of griddled asparagus with crispy Parma ham in spring or the earthy, filling comforts of braised red cabbage when the cold weather rolls in.

And what of our beloved potato? The perfect complete food! Whether you love the floury, old varieties of King Edward, Roosters or Maris Piper, baked and cracked open to reveal a fluffy cloud of potato. Or perhaps you prefer the elegant, almost creamy flavour of the waxy varieties of Jersey Royal, Cyprus and Charlotte that are so good in a gratin of potatoes. Either way you will love Superquinn's very own Oilean potato, a versatile floury spud that is grown in Ireland under special conditions to ensure perfect texture and freshness every time.

Italy on a PLATE

These chargrilled vegetables are very easy to prepare in advance ready to be cooked at the last minute. They are delicious served on their own or with some baked glazed ham (page 102).

Chargrilled Mediterranean vegetables with garlic cream

Serves 4

1 small garlic bulb, separated into cloves and peeled

about 4 tbsp cream, plus a little extra if necessary

4 tbsp milk

1 red and 1 yellow pepper, cored and cut into quarters

2 courgettes, trimmed and cut into thin slices lengthways

1 bunch asparagus, trimmed

1 large red onion, quartered and cut into wedges

3 tbsp olive oil

1 tsp balsamic vinegar

Maldon salt and freshly ground black pepper

fresh basil bush sprigs, to garnish (or use regular basil)

 To download the shopping list:
www.superquinn.ie/content/Chargrilled
MediterraneanVegetablesWithGarlicCream/909

Wine match
Mâcon-Villages
The subtleness of the Mâcon-Villages will highlight the creaminess of the garlic cream sauce whilst complimenting the freshness of the vegetables.

1 To make the garlic cream, place the garlic cloves in a small pan and cover with water. Bring to the boil and drain, then repeat this blanching and refresh under cold running water. Return the garlic to the pan and just cover with the cream and milk. Bring to a gentle simmer and cook for 6–8 minutes until the garlic is completely soft and the liquid has reduced slightly. Using a hand blender, blitz to a puree. Season to taste and set aside until needed.

2 Heat a griddle pan until smoking hot or light a barbecue. Place the peppers, courgettes, asparagus and red onion in a bowl and toss with the olive oil and balsamic vinegar. Season to taste. Arrange on the heated griddle pan or barbecue grill and cook for 6–10 minutes until cooked through and nicely marked, turning occasionally. You may have to do this in batches depending on the size of your pan and it's worth noting that each type of vegetable will take a slightly different time.

3 Warm the garlic cream, stirring occasionally and adding a little more cream if necessary until you have achieved a good sauce consistency. Arrange the chargrilled vegetables on warmed plates and drizzle around the garlic cream. Garnish with the basil bush sprigs to serve.

Chef's top tip –

If asparagus is not in season try using a fennel bulb instead. Simply trim down and cut into thin wedges before cooking with the rest of the vegetables.

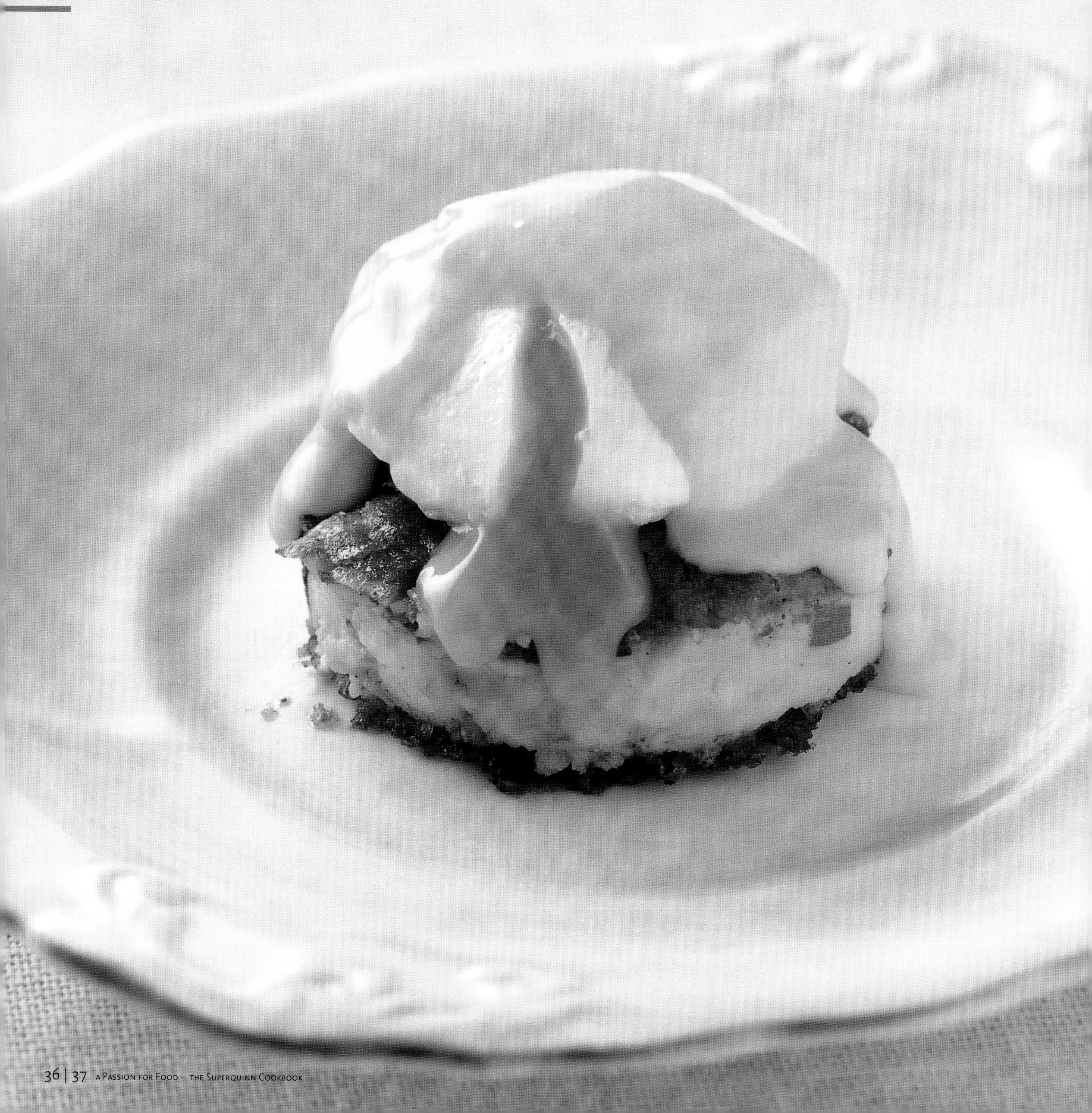

SMOOTH awakening

This dish would also be delicious served with a slice of baked ham (page 102) or bacon if you have any leftover. Alternatively, chop up the ham or bacon and add to the colcannon mixture before shaping into patties.

Colcannon cakes with poached eggs and hollandaise sauce

Serves 4

550 g (1 ¼ lb) potatoes, cut into chunks

about 40 g (1 ½ oz) butter

3 spring onions, finely chopped

50 g (2 oz) Savoy cabbage, shredded

a little plain flour, for dusting

2 tbsp olive oil

1 tbsp white wine vinegar

4 large eggs

For the hollandaise sauce:

2 tsp white wine vinegar

2 large egg yolks

100 g (4 oz) unsalted butter

Maldon sea salt and freshly cracked black pepper

Wine match
Australian Chardonnay
Dishes with runny eggs are often difficult to match a wine to but the crispness of a New World Chardonnay will help to cut through the egg for full flavour appreciation.

To download the shopping list:
www.superquinn.ie/content/ColcannonCakes
WithPoachedEggsAndHollandaiseSauce/910

1 Cook the potatoes in a covered pan of boiling salted water for 15–20 minutes until tender. Heat a knob of the butter and one tablespoon of water in a pan with a lid over a high heat. Once an emulsion has formed, add the spring onions and cabbage with a pinch of salt. Cover, shake vigorously and cook for 1 minute. Shake again and cook for another minute, then season with pepper.

2 Drain the potatoes and mash until smooth, then beat in the remaining butter. Fold in the cabbage mixture. Shape the mixture into four balls, dust with flour and press into patties. Heat the olive oil in a frying pan and add the patties, then cook for 3–4 minutes on each side until heated through and golden brown.

3 Meanwhile, bring a large pan of water to the boil. Add the vinegar and season with salt and keep at a gentle simmer. Break in the eggs and simmer for 3–4 minutes until just cooked but still soft on the inside. Remove with a slotted spoon and drain on kitchen paper, trimming away any ragged edges.

4 To make the hollandaise sauce, place the vinegar and egg yolks in a food processor with a pinch of salt. Blend until just combined. Heat the butter in a pan until melted and just beginning to foam. Turn on the food processor and pour in the melted butter in a thin, steady stream through the feeder tube. Blitz for another 5 seconds until nicely thickened. Season with salt. Arrange the colcannon cakes on warmed plates and top each one with a poached egg. Spoon over the hollandaise sauce to serve.

CUSTOMER RECIPE — TINA BRESCANU,
SUPERQUINN ONLINE

winterWARMER

Gratin of potatoes and cream with anchovies

"This dish reminds me of Christmas in Sweden when I was a child. It is a very popular dish known as Jansson's Temptation which has many different variations. However, the basic ingredients always stay the same. It is delicious served with all manner of meats but goes particularly well with a roast leg of lamb. Normally it is served with a glass of schnapps and a cold beer."

TINA is a busy mum who prefers to shop on Superquinn.ie, because it's a great way to stay on budget.

Serves 4

25 g (1 oz) butter, at room temperature

6 waxy potatoes (about 1 kg (2 ¼ lb) in total)

2 onions, thinly sliced (about 275 g (10 oz) in total)

50 g can anchovy fillets in extra virgin olive oil, drained and finely chopped

300 ml (½ pint) cream

3 tbsp fresh white breadcrumbs

Maldon sea salt and freshly ground back pepper

To download the shopping list: www.superquinn.ie/content/GratinOf PotatoesAndCreamWithAnchovies/911

1 Preheat the oven for 180°C (350°F), Gas mark 4. Generously butter a gratin dish. Peel and grate the potatoes and make layers of potato, onion and anchovy finishing with potatoes. Season as you go but be sparingly with the salt as the anchovies are quite salty anyway.

2 Press the potato mixture down firmly, then smooth over the surface and pour the cream on top so that the potatoes can be seen and are not smothered. Sprinkle over the breadcrumbs and dot with the rest of the butter. Cover with tin foil and bake for 1 hour until cooked through, then remove the foil and bake for another 10–15 minutes until bubbling and golden brown. Serve straight to the table.

Chef's top tip –

If you are short of time, try using the grating blade on a food processor to prepare the potatoes for you.

LEAFING
through

Butterhead lettuce leaves are thin and soft with a silky, almost buttery feel. They have a sweet, mild flavour with less prominent veins than iceberg and are great in light side salads. As they are grown in Ireland they can be on the supermarket shelf within 24 hours of being picked.

Butterhead lettuce salad with spring onions and tomatoes

Serves 4

6 streaky bacon rashers

1 head butterhead lettuce

100 g (4 oz) small plum or cherry tomatoes, cut into quarters

1 bunch spring onions, trimmed and chopped

3 tbsp extra virgin olive oil

1 tsp balsamic vinegar

2 tbsp finely chopped red onion

1 tbsp chopped fresh basil

Maldon sea salt and freshly ground black pepper

To download the shopping list:
www.superquinn.ie/content/Butterhead
LettuceSaladWithSpringOnionsAndTomatoes/912

Wine match
Sancerre
This light and fresh salad needs a zesty light white wine like a Sancerre to compliment not overpower the delicate flavours.

1 Preheat the grill and arrange the bacon on a grill rack. Cook for a couple of minutes on each side until crisp and lightly golden. Leave to cool on kitchen paper, then crumble into small pieces discarding any rinds.

2 Discard any outer damaged lettuce leaves and wash – a salad spinner is perfect, as it doesn't bruise the soft leaves. Break the lettuce leaves into a salad bowl and add the tomatoes, spring onions and the crumbled bacon.

3 Whisk the olive oil and balsamic vinegar in a small bowl. Stir in the red onion and basil, then season to taste. Drizzle over the salad and toss until lightly dressed. Serve immediately straight to the table.

Chef's top tip –

You can use this salad as a base and add quarters of hard-boiled eggs and/or anchovy fillets instead of the bacon. Some crunchy croutons will also be a great addition, whether they are shop-bought or homemade.

flat packed GOODNESS

These are fantastic served with some crusty bread to mop up all of the delicious juices but you could also serve them with a juicy steak and/or some garlic mash (page 105 and 106). Try to choose even-sized mushrooms with curled-up edges so that they hold the filling in place.

Baked field mushrooms with spinach, Gorgonzola and pine nuts

Serves 4

4 large flat breakfast mushrooms, trimmed

½ tsp chopped fresh thyme

2 garlic cloves, finely chopped

2 tbsp olive oil, plus a little extra

knob of butter

225 g (8 oz) spinach, washed and large stalks removed

150 g (5 oz) Gorgonzola cheese

2 tbsp pine nuts

Maldon sea salt and freshly ground black pepper

To download the shopping list:
www.superquinn.ie/content/BakedField
MushroomsWithSpinachGorgonzolaAnd
PineNuts/913

1 Preheat the oven to 200°C (400°F), Gas mark 6. Arrange the mushrooms, gill sides up in lightly oiled small roasting tin. Scatter over the thyme and garlic. Season to taste and drizzle over the olive oil. Cover the mushrooms loosely with tin foil and roast for 15 minutes until the mushrooms are just cooked through.

2 Melt the butter a large heavy-based pan and add fistfuls of the spinach, adding another as one wilts down. Cook for 1 minute, then tip into a colander and gently press out all the excess moisture.

3 Remove the foil from the mushrooms and divide the spinach among them. Season to taste, then dot over the Gorgonzola cheese and scatter the pine nuts on top, then drizzle over a little more olive oil.

4 Return the stuffed mushrooms to the oven and roast for another 4–5 minutes or until the spinach is heated through and the cheese is bubbling. Transfer each mushroom to a warmed plate and spoon over the pan juices to serve.

Chef's top tip –

For a great vegetarian option for the barbecue, sandwich together the spinach filling between two mushrooms and brush liberally with olive oil. Cook on the barbecue over medium coals for 10–12 minutes, turning occasionally until the musshrooms are cooked through and tender.

Wine match
White Burgundy
The crispness of a White Burgundy is a perfect companion for the earthy mushrooms and spinach.

statement BAG

These carrots not only taste delicious but also are the perfect accompaniment to any roast, such as the roast rib of beef (page 94) or the roast chicken (page 110). The best part is that they can be prepared well in advance leaving nothing to do at the last minute, except of course remembering to pop them in the oven!

Baked carrot batons in a bag with thyme

Serves 4–6

800 g (1 lb 12 oz) carrots

1 large shallot, finely chopped

2 garlic cloves, finely chopped

1 tsp fresh thyme leaves

40 g (1 ½ oz) butter

Maldon sea salt and freshly ground black pepper

To download the shopping list:
www.superquinn.ie/content/BakedCarrot
BatonsInABagWithThyme/914

1 Preheat the oven to 180°C (350°F), Gas mark 4. Peel and trim the carrots and then cut into even-sized batons. Take a large double sheet of parchment paper or use a single sheet of tin foil and pile the carrot batons in the middle.

2 Scatter the shallot, garlic and thyme over the carrots and dot with the butter, then drizzle over two tablespoons of water. Season to taste, then fold in the sides of the parcel to enclose the carrots by bringing up the sides, then folding over and twisting the edges.

3 Place the parchment bag on a baking sheet and roast for 1 hour until the carrots are meltingly tender and slightly caramelised. To serve, either open the parchment parcel at the table or carefully pour the carrots and all of their juices into a nice big warmed dish.

Chef's top tip —

The oven temperature for these carrots is quite flexible so simply put on the bottom shelf of your oven depending on what roast you are cooking and adjust the cooking time accordingly.

CASTING
asparagus

This delicious starter is best eaten during asparagus season, which runs for approximately eight weeks in May and June. This is when they are at their best with a full, sweet flavour and fine, tender texture.

Griddled asparagus with crispy pancetta and soft boiled eggs

Serves 4

20 asparagus spears

20 thin slices pancetta (Italian streaky bacon)

1 tbsp olive oil

4 large eggs

15 g (½ oz) butter

Maldon sea salt and freshly ground black pepper

 **To download the shopping list:**
www.superquinn.ie/content/GriddledAsparagus
WithCrispyPancettaAndSoftBoiledEggs/915

Wine match
New Zealand Chardonnay
The crisp acidity matches perfectly with the asparagus whilst the creaminess works well with the egg.

Chef's top tip —

Before cooking the eggs, prick the wide end of each one with a pin, this will release the air trapped in a little pocket here and stop the eggs from cracking while they cook.

1 Trim the asparagus spears and then blanch in a pan of boiling water for 1–2 minutes until almost tender but still with a slight bite.

2 Drain the asparagus spears and quickly refresh under cold running water, then pat dry on kitchen paper. Wrap each of the asparagus spears in a slice of pancetta and arrange on a plate. Drizzle with the olive oil and season to taste.

3 Meanwhile, heat a griddle pan until very hot. Bring a pan of water to the boil. Gently lower in the eggs and cook for 4 ½ minutes, turning them over once or twice during cooking.

4 Add the wrapped asparagus spears to the heated griddle pan and cook for 2–3 minutes until crisp and lightly golden, turning regularly.

5 Put the boiled eggs into eggcups and then carefully crack off the tops. Add a small knob of butter into each one and season to taste. Arrange on plates with the griddled asparagus with crispy pancetta stacked to the side to serve.

EARTHY delights

Sweet potatoes are very different to regular potatoes that we are used to in Ireland, but they are equally delicious. They are normally purple so they need to be peeled to uncover the wonderful orange-coloured flesh underneath.

Sweet potato soup with coconut and chilli

Serves 4

2 tbsp sunflower oil

1 large onion, finely chopped

1 cm (½ in) piece fresh root ginger, peeled and grated (about 2 tsp)

1 red chilli, seeded and finely chopped

675 g (1 ½ lb) sweet potatoes, peeled and cut into cubes

400 g can coconut milk

600 ml (1 pint) chicken or vegetable stock

salt and freshly ground black pepper

To download the shopping list:
www.superquinn.ie/content/SweetPotato
SoupWithCoconutAndChilli/916

1 Heat the sunflower oil in a pan. Add the onion, ginger and chilli and sauté for 3–4 minutes until the onion has softened, stirring occasionally. Add the sweet potatoes and continue to sauté for 6–8 minutes until just tender and beginning to colour.

2 Pour the coconut milk into the pan with the stock and bring to the boil. Then reduce the heat and simmer for 10–15 minutes or until the liquid has slightly reduced and the sweet potatoes are completely tender.

3 Season to taste and then blitz with a hand blender until smooth. Ladle the soup into warmed bowls to serve.

Chef's top tip –

If you are entertaining, try dusting rings of baby squid with cornflour before deep-frying them until crisp. Add a squeeze of lemon and use as a garnish. They really transform the soup into something quite special.

Wine match
Australian Sauvignon Semillion Blend
The fruit and breadth in this blend of wine compliments the Thai flavours of this dish perfectly.

greater PAN

Risotto is a great dish for entertaining friends and should take no more than about 30 minutes from start to finish. The secret to success for a perfect risotto every time is to start by using a good quality heavy-based, shallow pan that distributes the heat evenly – a sauté pan is perfect.

Butternut squash risotto with sage

Serves 4-6

4 tbsp olive oil

800 g (1 lb 12 oz) butternut squash, peeled, seeded and finely diced

4 tbsp finely shredded fresh sage

1 large onion, finely chopped

2 garlic cloves, crushed

500 g packet carnavoli risotto rice

about 1.75 litres (3 pints) chicken or vegetable stock

300 ml (½ pint) dry white wine

25 g (1 oz) butter, diced

50 g (2 oz) freshly grated Parmesan, plus extra to garnish

1 tbsp snipped fresh chives

salt and freshly ground black pepper

Wine match
Australian Viognier
The full flavour of the Australian Viognier matches the hint of sweetness in the butternut squash.

To download the shopping list:
www.superquinn.ie/content/ButternutSquash RisottoWithSage/917

1. Heat a heavy-based sauté pan with half the olive oil. Add the butternut squash with the sage and mix well to combine. Season to taste and cook over a gentle heat for 8–10 minutes, stirring occasionally until the butternut squash is cooked through but still holding its shape. Transfer to a plate and set aside.

2. Add the rest of the olive oil to the pan and then tip in the onion and garlic and cook gently for 3–4 minutes until softened, stirring occasionally. Increase the heat, stir in the rice and cook gently for 1 minute, stirring continuously, until the rice is opaque and perfumed.

3. Meanwhile, pour the stock into a separate pan and bring to a gentle simmer. Pour the wine into the rice mixture and allow it to bubble away, stirring regularly. Add a ladleful of stock and cook gently, stirring, until absorbed. Continue to add the simmering stock a ladleful at a time, stirring frequently. Allow each stock addition to be almost completely absorbed before adding the next ladleful, until the rice is 'al dente' – tender with a slight bite. This should take 18 minutes.

4. Carefully fold in the butternut squash with the butter, Parmesan and chives, then season to taste. Leave to rest and swell a little more for 3 minutes. Ladle into wide-rimmed warmed bowls and scatter with Parmesan and freshly ground black pepper to serve.

give BRAISE

This would be delicious with honey roast duck breasts (page 108) or glazed ham (page 102) and serve with baked jacket potatoes with a dollop of soured cream and chives. The easiest way to cut the red cabbage and onions is on a Japanese mandolin but of course you can do it with a sharp knife if you don't have one.

Braised red cabbage with pomegranate

Serves 4 – 6

4 tbsp duck or goose fat (from a jar)

1 red cabbage, trimmed, stalks removed and finely shredded

2 red onions, thinly sliced

1 large Bramley cooking apple, peeled, cored and grated

300 ml (½ pint) pomegranate juice

4 tbsp red wine vinegar

2 tbsp redcurrant jelly

¼ tsp ground cinnamon

good pinch of ground cloves

salt and freshly ground black pepper

To download the shopping list:
www.superquinn.ie/content/BraisedRedCabbage
WithPomegranate/918

1 Heat a very large heavy-based pan. Add the duck or goose fat and once it has melted, tip in the red cabbage and onions. Sauté over a medium to high heat for about 5 minutes until just beginning to soften.

2 Stir the apple into the cabbage mixture and then add the pomegranate juice, red wine vinegar, redcurrant jelly and spices. Bring to the boil, stirring occasionally, then reduce the heat and simmer for about 1 hour, stirring every 20 minutes until the cabbage is meltingly tender. Transfer to a warmed dish and serve at once.

Chef's top tip —

Any leftovers can be kept in the fridge for a couple of days and then reheated. Alternatively this red cabbage freezes very well, simply pop into medium sized freezer bags and leave to thaw out before reheating gently either on the hob or in a casserole dish with a lid in the oven.

on the WEDGE

These are perfect for a party or barbecue but take the pressure off and bake in roasting tins in the oven. They're always a winner, especially with children and you'll probably find that you can never make enough!

Tangy tomato potato wedges with soured cream & chive dip

Serves 4 – 6

1.5 kg (3 lb) large Oilean potatoes

4 tbsp olive oil

2 tbsp tomato purée

1 tbsp Cajun seasoning

2 tsp sweet paprika

200 ml carton soured cream

2 tbsp snipped fresh chives, plus little extra to garnish

Maldon sea salt and freshly ground black pepper

To download the shopping list:
www.superquinn.ie/content/TangyTomato
PotatoWedgesWithSouredCream&ChiveDip/919

1 Preheat the oven to 200°C (400°F), Gas mark 6. Scrub the potatoes and cut each one into 6–8 even-sized wedges, depending on their size. Place the potatoes in a pan of boiling water, return to the boil and blanch for 2–3 minutes, then drain.

2 Put the olive oil in a large bowl with a teaspoon of the salt and the tomato purée, Cajun seasoning and paprika, stirring to combine. Add the wedges and toss until well coated, then arrange them in rows 'sitting' upright on their skins in two roasting tins. Bake for 35–40 minutes until completely tender and lightly golden, changing the oven shelves halfway through to ensure they cook evenly.

3 To make the dip; place the soured cream in a bowl and stir in the chives and season to taste. Cover with cling film and chill until ready to use. When the wedges are cooked, pile them on to a large warmed platter with the soured cream dip to the side and garnish with a little extra freshly ground black pepper and chives to serve.

Wine match
New Zealand Sauvignon Blanc
The fruitiness of the New Zealand Sauvignon Blanc will accentuate the tangy yet spicy flavours in this dish.

the DELI

TASTE
at your
fingertips

THE DELI

Lighten your load and give yourself a break with some clever shopping for delicious deli treats. Stock up on the quality Irish smoked salmon for a carpaccio with horseradish cream, served with Sean's brown bread. Or simply lay out a platter with some bruschetta and an array of continental meats and delicious antipasti.

For impressive entertaining why not present your guests with crisp filo baskets with black pudding and Cashel blue or some Parma ham with griddled figs and soft goat's cheese. For a short-cut dinner pick up a cooked Irish chicken from the rotisserie to make some mouthwatering chicken chilli tortillas with harrisa dressing. And don't forget about the Italian-style sausage rolls that will disappear in minutes. Whatever the occasion there is a no fuss feast that is perfect whatever the occasion.

A fresh START

This deliciously informal antipasti platter looks absolutely stunning when served like this. The whole thing can be prepared from start to finish in a matter of minutes: perfect for a summer supper or to serve as nibbles before a long lazy Sunday lunch.

Antipasti platter with bruschetta

Serves 4

6 slices Parma ham

75 g (3 oz) sun-dried cherry tomatoes, drained (from a jar)

75 g (3 oz) marinated black olives, drained

25 g (1 oz) wild rocket

½ tsp balsamic vinegar

1 tbsp extra virgin olive oil

For the artichoke dip:

285 g jar marinated artichoke hearts in oil, well drained

100 g (4 oz) feta cheese, roughly chopped

1 tbsp fresh lemon juice

3 tbsp olive oil, plus extra for drizzling

Maldon sea salt and freshly ground black pepper

bruschetta, to serve

To download the shopping list:
www.superquinn.ie/content/AntipastiPlatter
WithBruschetta/920

1   To make the artichoke dip, place the drained artichoke hearts in a food processor with the feta and lemon juice. Blitz to form a smooth paste and then with the motor running, slowly add the olive oil until well combined. Season to taste and spoon into a serving bowl.

2   Set the bowl of artichoke dip on a large platter and drizzle over a little more olive oil, then season with pepper. Arrange the slices of Parma ham on the platter with nice loose mounds of the sun-dried cherry tomatoes and olives. Tip the rocket into a bowl and dress with the extra virgin olive oil and balsamic vinegar. Season to taste and pile on to the platter with a stack of the bruschetta to serve.

Chef's top tip –

Don't be tempted to make bruschetta too far in advance, as the bread goes soggy. Preheat a cast-iron griddle pan and brush slices of French stick with seasoned olive oil. Cook for a minute or two on each side until lightly charred and then rub one side with a halved garlic clove.

Wine match
Italian Pinot Grigio
The freshness of the Italian Pinot Grigio was made for Antipasti!

rockin' ROLLS

These sausage rolls will delight your guests with their moreish flavours. Add the best quality ingredients and you have a guilt-free winner for party food.

Italian-style sausage rolls

Chef's top tip –

These sausage rolls can be frozen uncooked for up to one month. Layer up between sheets of parchment paper in a plastic rigid container and secure with a lid before freezing. Increase the cooking time by about 10 minutes if cooking straight from frozen.

Wine match
Chianti
Italian Chianti is a medium bodied red and so matches the flavour of the sausage and sun-dried tomato without overpowering.

Makes 16 small sausage rolls

500 g packet sausage meat

1 small onion, finely chopped

50 g (2 oz) sun-dried tomatoes in oil, drained and finely chopped

3 tbsp chopped fresh flat-leaf parsley

4 tbsp freshly grated Parmesan

500 g packet frozen puff pastry, thawed

1 egg, beaten

plain flour, for dusting

salt and freshly ground black pepper

To download the shopping list:
www.superquinn.ie/content/ItalianStyle
SausageRolls/921

1 Preheat the oven to 200°C (400°F), Gas mark 6. To make the filling, mix the sausage meat in a bowl with the onion, sun-dried tomatoes, parsley and Parmesan. Season to taste.

2 Cut the pastry in half and roll out one piece on a lightly floured surface to make a long oblong shape, 35 x 17 cm (16 x 6 ½ in). Form half of the filling into a long log-shape that will run the whole length of the pastry, approximately 5 mm (¼ in) from the edge. Brush with beaten egg, then fold the pastry over to enclose the filling and press down well to seal the edges, either crimping them with your fingers or pressing down with a fork. Repeat with the rest of the pastry and filling.

3 Cut long sausage roll into 8 bite-sized pieces, trimming down and discarding the ends. Brush with beaten egg to glaze and arrange on two baking sheets lined with parchment paper. Bake for 15–20 minutes until cooked through and lightly golden, swapping the baking sheets around on the oven shelves half way through. Arrange on plates or a large platter and serve hot or cold.

CUSTOMER RECIPE — CLARA CLIFFORD,
SUPERQUINN NORTHSIDE

good EGG

Italian frittata

"This Italian-style omelette is called a frittata in Italy and is delicious hot or cold. It is cooked until set firm, making it excellent picnic food or as an addition to a platter of antipasti, as well as a light lunch or supper."

Serves 4

8 large eggs, beaten

50 g (2 oz) hard cheese, finely grated (such as Cheddar, Emmental or Gruyère)

100 g (4 oz) cooked ham or loin of bacon, cut into cubes

1 tbsp chopped fresh flat-leaf parsley

1 tbsp olive oil

salt and freshly ground black pepper

lightly dressed green salad, to serve

Wine match
Italian Pinot Grigio
The light flavours of this dish call for a light unoaked Pinot Grigio from the North of Italy.

To download the shopping list:
www.superquinn.ie/content/ItalianFrittata/922

1 Lightly beat the eggs in a large bowl with one tablespoon of water and add most of the cheese, then fold in the cooked ham or bacon and parsley. Season to taste.

2 Heat a frying pan with the oil. Swirl to coat the sides of the pan evenly, then pour in the egg mixture and cook for 1 minute. Reduce the heat to low and use a fork or wooden spatula to draw the mixture from the sides to the centre as it sets. Cook for another 3–4 minutes to set the bottom and sides.

3 Meanwhile, preheat the grill. When the eggs have almost set, scatter over the remaining cheese, then flash the frittata under the grill until just cooked through and lightly golden. Leave to settle in the pan for a few minutes before cutting into wedges and arranging on plates with the salad to serve.

CLARA shops in Superquinn Northside and loves the fresh smell of bread that greets her at the door. She is particularly fond of the brown bread for her breakfast in the morning.

it's a WRAP

This is a great recipe for using leftover roast chicken, but a shop-bought cooked chicken from the deli counter also works well.

Chicken chilli tortillas with harissa dressing

Serves 4

1 cooked chicken

200 g (7 oz) jar natural yoghurt

1 tbsp harissa (hot chilli paste – from a jar)

2 tbsp olive oil

1 large red onion, cut into thin slices

1 red and 1 yellow pepper, cored and cut into thin slices

8 soft flour tortillas

50 g (2 oz) crisp green lettuce, shredded

Maldon sea salt and freshly ground black pepper

To download the shopping list:
www.superquinn.ie/content/ChickenChilli
TortillasWithHarissaDressing/923

1 Strip the meat off the bones of the chicken and shred or cut into smallish, bite-sized chunks – you'll need 450 g (1 lb) in total. To make the dressing, place the yoghurt in a bowl and mix in the harissa, then season to taste.

2 Heat the olive oil in a sauté pan. Add the red onion and peppers and then season to taste. Sauté for about 10 minutes until lightly golden but the peppers are still holding their crunch.

3 Heat a separate frying pan and quickly toast each flour tortilla for 10–20 seconds on each side. Place a line of lettuce down each tortilla and spoon the onion and pepper mixture on top. Add the chicken and then drizzle over the harissa dressing. Roll up each tortilla before cutting on the diagonal and arrange on plates to serve.

Chef's top tip –

You could also use breaded chicken fillets or goujons that you pan-fry and thinly slice for this recipe.

Wine match
Chilean Sauvignon Blanc
The fruitiness of the Chilean Sauvignon compliments the heat from the chilli and lightness of the chicken and yoghurt-based dressing.

pâté EVER AFTER

This chicken liver pâté is full of gutsy flavours and is a wonderful starter or you could spread on crackers and hand around as a nibble.

Chicken liver pâté with balsamic vinegar

Serves 4 – 6

1 tbsp olive oil

100 g (4 oz) unsalted butter

1 small onion, finely chopped

2 garlic cloves, finely chopped

1 tsp fresh thyme leaves

450 g (1 lb) chicken livers, well cleaned and trimmed

3 tbsp balsamic vinegar

4 anchovy fillets, finely chopped (from a can or jar, drained)

1 tbsp capers, rinsed

2 tbsp chopped fresh flat-leaf parsley

salt and freshly ground black pepper

lightly dressed rocket leaves and crostini, to serve

Wine match
New Zealand Pinot Noir
Red wine can be an unusual choice here but the softness of the Pinot Noir compliments both the the pâté and balsamic.

To download the shopping list:
www.superquinn.ie/content/ChickenLiver
PateWithBalsamicVinegar/924

1 Heat the oil and 25 g (1 oz) of the butter in a non-stick frying pan until foaming. Add the onion, garlic and thyme and gently fry for about 5 minutes until the onion has softened but not coloured. Increase the heat and add the chicken livers. Fry for 4–5 minutes, turning constantly until lightly golden but still pink in the middle.

2 Tip the contents of the pan into a food processor and then return the pan to the heat. Add the balsamic vinegar and stir vigorously to release any sediment. Allow to reduce by half and then tip into the food processor with the anchovy fillets, capers, parsley and seasoning, then pulse until it is almost smooth but still has a bit of texture.

3 Leave the chicken liver pâté to cool completely then spoon into individual ramekins. Melt the rest of the butter in a pan or in the microwave, leave to settle, then use to cover each ramekin of pâté, leaving the sediment behind. Cover with cling film and chill for at least 2 hours or overnight is best. Remove from the fridge 30 minutes before you want to serve them. Place each ramekin on a plate and add a small pile of the rocket leaves to one side, then arrange a stack of crostini on each plate to serve.

Chef's top tip –

This also freezes very well; cover tightly with cling film and thaw out at room temperature before using.

salmon
of KNOWLEDGE

This is a wonderfully impressive starter that is actually incredibly easy to make. It would also work well on a large platter as part of a buffet.

Smoked salmon carpaccio with horseradish cream

Serves 4

400 g packet thinly sliced smoked salmon

1 small ripe avocado

1 cooked beetroot (vacuum-packed)

3 tbsp soured cream

1 tbsp creamed horseradish

1 tsp Dijon mustard

pinch of sugar

2 tbsp snipped fresh chives

1 tsp fresh dill fronds

salt and freshly ground white pepper

thin slices of Sean's brown bread, to serve

To download the shopping list:
www.superquinn.ie/content/SmokedSalmonCarpaccio
WithHorseradishCream/925

1 Trim the smoked salmon slices of any dark pieces and arrange on flat plates in a slightly overlapping layer.

2 Cut the avocado in half, then remove the stone and carefully peel away the skin. Cut the flesh into 5 mm (¼ in) dice. Cut the beetroot into identical sized dice, then scatter both over the smoked salmon slices.

3 Place the soured cream in a bowl and beat in the creamed horseradish, mustard and sugar, then season to taste. Dot over the smoked salmon carpaccio and sprinkle over the chives and dill. Season with pepper and add slices of Sean's brown bread to serve.

Wine match
Californian Chardonnay
The gentle smoked oak tones of the Californian Chardonnay are perfect with smoked salmon.

The PUFF daddy

These puff pizza tarts not only look stunning but also are delicious to eat. If the pastry puffs up during the cooking time simply push back down by rubbing the back of a spoon over the centre to flatten completely.

Mediterranean vegetable puff pizza tart

Serves 4

500 g packet puff pastry, thawed

plain flour, for dusting

1 small red pepper and 1 yellow pepper

3 tbsp olive oil

beaten egg, for glazing

1 small courgette

1 red onion

1 small aubergine

2 egg yolks, lightly beaten

120 ml (4 fl oz) cream

175 g (6 oz) taleggio cheese, rind removed and diced

Maldon sea salt and freshly ground black pepper

To download the shopping list:
www.superquinn.ie/content/ Mediterranean VegetablePuffPizzaTart/926

1. Cut the pastry into four pieces and roll out each one slightly larger than a 20 cm (8 in) square on a lightly floured board, then trim down the edges. Using a sharp knife, mark out a rim about 1 cm (½ in) wide, then arrange on large baking sheets and chill for 30 minutes.

2. Meanwhile, preheat the oven to 190°C (375°F), Gas mark 5 and preheat the grill. Rub the peppers with a little of the oil and roast them under the grill for 20 minutes until the skins are blackened and blistered, turning regularly. Transfer to a bowl and cover with cling film, then leave to cool. Peel, seed and cut into 5 mm (¼ in) dice. Cut the courgette, red onion and aubergine into the same size.

3. Brush the pastry bases with beaten egg, being careful not to let it run down the outer edge of the pastry as this will prevent it from rising and prick the bases inside the rims to prevent them from puffing up. Bake for about 15 minutes, until puffed up and lightly golden, swapping the baking sheets around on the oven shelves half way through.

4. Meanwhile, heat the rest of the olive oil in a frying pan and sauté the courgette, red onion and aubergine on a medium heat for 8–10 minutes until the vegetables are just tender. Season to taste and stir in the roasted peppers.

5. Place the egg yolks in a bowl with the cream. Lightly beat to combine, then stir in the cooked Mediterranean vegetables. Spoon the vegetable mixture into the pastry bases inside the rims and sprinkle the taleggio on top. Return to the oven for 15 minutes or until the vegetable mixture is just set and the cheese is bubbling. Arrange on warmed plates to serve.

Chef's top tip –
You can also use Parmesan cheese instead of the taleggio cheese if you prefer.

Wine match
Beaujolais
Mediterranean vegetables are at the best when complimented with a light fruity red wine like Beaujolais.

PUD
intentions

This is a delicious salad that's packed full of flavour. Don't be tempted to overcook the black pudding; it needs no more than a minute on each side. It would also be fantastic with a poached egg on top.

Bacon and spinach salad with black pudding

Serves 4

4 tbsp extra virgin olive oil

175 g (6 oz) black pudding, skinned and cut into 1cm (½ in) slices

4 maple cured bacon rashers

175 g (6 oz) mixed salad leaves (such as baby spinach and rocket)

1 ripe avocado

2 tsp white wine vinegar

1 tsp wholegrain mustard

½ tsp clear honey

salt and freshly ground black pepper

crusty bread, to serve

Wine match
Valpolicella
The black pudding in this dish calls for a light juicy red like Valpolicella.

To download the shopping list:
www.superquinn.ie/content/BaconAndSpinach
SaladWithBlackPudding/927

1 Heat a frying pan and then add a tablespoon of olive oil. Add the black pudding and cook for 1 minute on each side until tender. Transfer to a plate and keep warm.

2 Snip the bacon into the frying pan and sauté for a few minutes until sizzling and lightly golden.

3 Meanwhile, place the salad leaves in a large bowl. Halve, stone and chop the avocado. Add to the bowl and season to taste.

4 Using a slotted spoon, remove the bacon from the pan and add to the salad. Pour the vinegar into the pan, turn up the heat and scrape the sediment in the pan with a wooden spoon to deglaze until almost all the vinegar has been boiled off.

5 Stir the mustard into the reduced down vinegar with the honey and then whisk in the rest of the olive oil until you have achieved a nice emulsion.

6 Break the black pudding up into pieces and scatter over the salad, then drizzle over the dressing. Toss lightly to combine and then arrange on plates to serve. Hand around a basket of crusty bread separately.

This is a great starter for a dinner party. Filo pastry is available from the frozen section. It is important to keep it covered with a damp tea towel while you are working with it to prevent it from drying out.

upper CASE

Filo baskets with black pudding and Cashel Blue

Serves 4

50 g (2 oz) butter

3 sheets filo pastry, thawed

1 tsp sunflower oil

275 g (10 oz) black pudding, casing removed and cut into slices

1 red-skinned eating apple, cored and diced

a knob of butter

about 4 tbsp red onion marmalade

150 g (5 oz) Cashel Blue cheese

fresh whole chives, to garnish

lightly dressed salad, to serve

To download the shopping list:
www.superquinn.ie/content/FiloBaskets
WithBlackPuddingAndCashelBlue/928

Wine match
Argentine Malbec
The strong flavours of the blue cheese and black pudding call for a more full bodied red such as the Argentine Malbec.

1 Preheat the oven to 180°C (350°F), Gas mark 4. Melt the butter in a small pan or in the microwave, then leave to cool a little. Unfold the filo pastry and cut the sheets into quarters, then cover with a damp tea towel. Take 4 x 200 ml (7 fl oz) glass ramekins and turn upside down on a non-stick baking sheet.

2 Take a piece of the filo pastry and brush one side with butter, then use to cover the top of the ramekin, buttered side down. Add another two layers of the brushed filo pastry, placing each rectangle at a slightly different angle. Repeat until you have four covered ramekins in total, then tuck in the edges. Bake for 10–12 minutes until lightly golden. When cool enough to handle remove the filo baskets from the ramekins, then transfer to a wire rack to cool.

3 Heat a heavy-based frying pan with the sunflower oil and sauté the black pudding for a minute or so on each side until lightly crisp. Drain on kitchen paper. Add the apple to the pan with the butter and sauté for a couple of minutes until tender and lightly coloured. Break up the black pudding and toss to combine.

4 Add a spoonful of the onion marmalade into each filo basket and spoon the black pudding and apple mixture on top. Crumble over largish chunks of the Cashel Blue and put on a baking sheet. Bake for another 5 minutes until the Cashel Blue has just melted. Arrange on plates with the salad and finish each one with a teaspoon of the onion marmalade and garnish with chives to serve.

go FIG

The combination of figs and Parma ham is hard to beat. This simple, yet stylish starter or light supper is perfect for a summers evening. You can substitute the goats cheese with Dolcelatte or Gorgonzola with excellent results.

Parma ham with griddled figs and soft goat's cheese

Serves 4

6 ripe figs

4 tbsp extra virgin olive oil

1 tbsp clear honey

200 g (7 oz) soft goat's cheese, broken into chunks

12 slices Parma ham

100 g (4 oz) watercress, woody stems removed

1 tsp balsamic vinegar

Maldon sea salt and freshly ground black pepper

To download the shopping list:
www.superquinn.ie/content/ParmaHam
WithGriddledFigsAndSoftGoatsCheese/929

1 Heat a griddle pan. Halve the figs and brush with a mixture of one tablespoon of the olive oil and the honey. Arrange on the griddle pan; cut side down over a medium-low heat for 3 minutes. The figs should be soft and caramelised with attractive grill markings.

2 Arrange the griddled figs, goat's cheese, Parma ham and watercress on plates. Drizzle with the rest of the olive oil and the balsamic vinegar, and season to taste. Serve at room temperature.

Wine match
New Zealand Sauvignon Blanc
The ripeness of the New Zealand Sauvignon is a perfect match for goat's cheese and will really amplify the fruitiness of the figs.

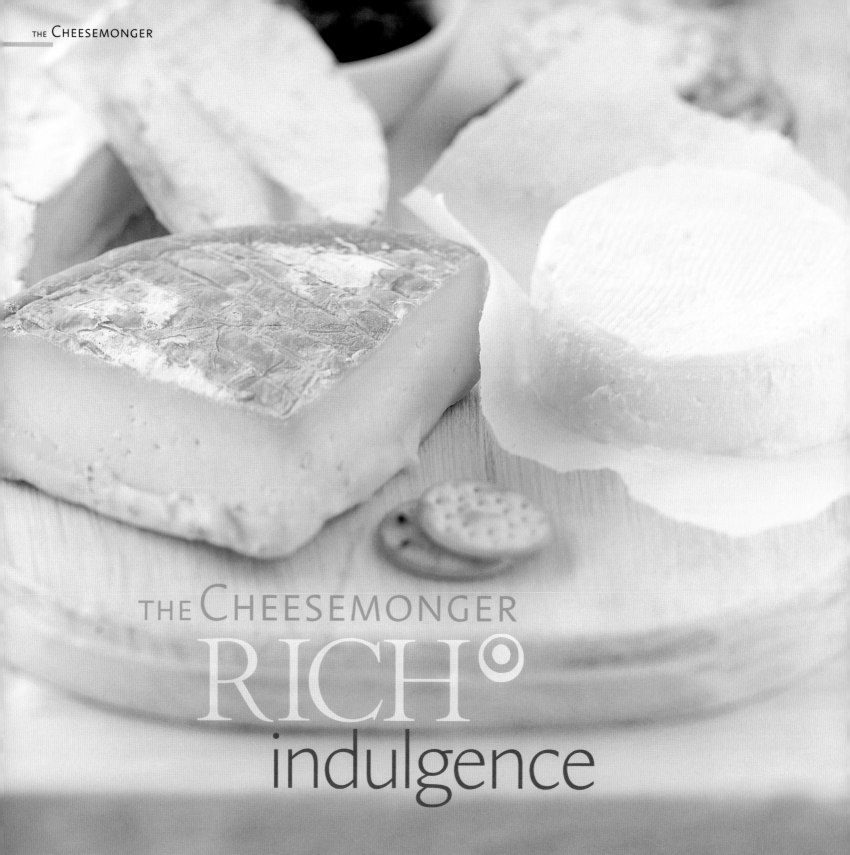

THE CHEESEMONGER
RICH°
indulgence

THE CHEESEMONGER

There are so many flavours, textures, finishes and moods of cheese. It is one of those perfect foods that no cook should be without. It can add the final flourish to a simple salad, enrich a bake, improve a tart, thicken a sauce, add a treat to toast and end a meal with come-back-for-more applause.

From a crumbly, hard slice of mature cheddar to a tangy, nutty blue veined creamy cheese or a snow-white slice of soft goat's cheese to an oozing, wedge of Camembert or Brie, there is so much to enjoy. And let's not forget the pure pleasure of gently melting Buffalo mozzarella or the moreish savoury hit of roughly grated fresh Parmesan.

In Ireland we produce some of the finest farmhouse cheeses in the world and you'll find the largest range at Superquinn. If you haven't yet indulged in the savoury perfection of a mature Coolea farmhouse Gouda or the salty, creamy Bellingham Blue from Co Louth, or Mary Burns' washed rind semi-soft Ardrahan – you are in for a real treat just ask your local Superquinn cheesemonger for the size you want.

TARTgallery

These mini-tartlets are the ultimate finger food at parties: easy to prepare in advance and with a melt in the mouth taste. Experiment with different soft cheeses or try adding some sautéed diced bacon.

Goat's cheese and caramelised onion tartlets with thyme

Makes 12

2 tbsp olive oil, plus a little extra

2 large onions, finely chopped

1 large egg yolk

3 tbsp cream

200 g goats' cheese log with rind

½ tsp fresh thyme leaves

For the pastry:

175 g (6 oz) plain flour, plus extra for dusting

75 g (3 oz) butter, cut into cubes (at room temperature)

40 g (1 ½ oz) freshly grated Parmesan

good pinch of cayenne pepper, plus extra for dusting

1 large egg, beaten

salt and freshly ground white pepper

Wine match
Chilean Sauvignon Blanc
Zippy acidity compliments the cheese whilst the fruit works really well with the caramelised onion

To download the shopping list:
www.superquinn.ie/content/GoatsCheeseAnd CaramelisedOnionTartletsWithThyme/930

1   First make the pastry. Sieve the flour into a bowl, then add the butter. Take a knife and begin to cut it into the flour until it looks fairly evenly blended. Add the Parmesan and cayenne with just enough cold water to make a smooth dough mixture (about 5 tablespoons), before discarding the knife and bringing it together with your fingertips. Place in a plastic food bag and put it into the fridge to rest for at least 30 minutes.

2   Preheat the oven to 180°C (350°F), Gas mark 4. Roll out the pastry to a 5 mm (¼ in) thickness on a lightly floured work surface. Use a 7.5 cm (3 in) cutter to stamp out 12 rounds and use to line a bun tin, then scrunch up small balls of tin foil and use to fill the pastry cases to help them stay in shape. Bake for about 10 minutes until cooked through and lightly golden.

3   Heat the olive oil in a frying pan and cook the onions for about 1 hour until caramelised, stirring regularly to prevent the bottom from catching. Season to taste and leave to cool, then spoon a little into each pastry case.

4   Whisk the egg yolk and cream in a jug and season. Pour over the caramelised onions. Cut the goat's cheese log into 12 thin slices and use to top each tartlet, then sprinkle over the thyme and drizzle with a little olive oil. Bake for 10–12 minutes or until lightly golden and set. Arrange on a platter on squares of parchment paper and dust with cayenne. Serve warm or at room temperature.

FRENCH. connection

You could use ordinary ham in this recipe or replace the Gruyére with Cheddar depending on what you fancy.

Leeks wrapped in Parma ham with Gruyére

Serves 4

8 small leeks, well trimmed

16 slices Parma ham

butter, for greasing

150 g (5 oz) Gruyére cheese, grated

2 tbsp Dijon mustard

6 tbsp crème fraîche

crusty French bread, to serve

 To download the shopping list:
www.superquinn.ie/content/LeeksWrapped
InParmaHamWithGruyere/931

Wine match
Australian Chardonnay
The buttery tones of the Australian Chardonnay lift the flavour of the Parma ham and match the power of the Gruyére cheese.

1 Preheat the oven to 200°C (400°F), Gas mark 6. Blanch the leeks in a pan of boiling salted water for 3–4 minutes or until just tender. Drain and quickly refresh under cold running water to stop them from cooking any further, then drain well and pat dry on kitchen paper.

2 Wrap each leek in two slices of Parma ham and arrange them in a buttered baking dish. Place the Gruyére in a bowl and stir in the Dijon mustard and crème fraîche until well combined. Season to taste. Spread over the leeks and bake for 15–20 minutes until bubbling and golden brown. Serve at once straight to the table with plenty of crusty bread to mop up all of those delicious juices.

Louth and PROUD

Bellingham Blue is a creamy blue veined award winning Irish cheese, handmade in Louth from a herd of Friesian cows. As an unpasteurised cheese it has a distinct tangy, almost nutty flavour with a slight hint of fruit.

Salad of Bellingham Blue, pears and walnuts

Serves 4

½ tsp white wine vinegar

1 tsp Dijon mustard

3 tbsp extra virgin olive oil

3 chicory heads, leaves separated

50 g (2 oz) baby spinach leaves

1 firm ripe pear, cored and thinly sliced

8 shelled walnuts, roughly chopped

250 g (9 oz) Bellingham Blue, roughly crumbled (unpasteurised)

Maldon sea salt and freshly ground black pepper

To download the shopping list:
www.superquinn.ie/content/SaladOfBellingham
BluePearsAndWalnuts/932

1 To make the dressing, whisk the vinegar, mustard and olive oil in a small bowl, adding a little water if the dressing becomes too thick.

2 Toss the chicory and spinach together and arrange on plates, then season to taste. Scatter over the pear, walnuts and Bellingham Blue. Drizzle the dressing on top and serve at once.

Chef's top tip –

This salad would also be delicious with some crunchy croutons. Toss cubes of rustic bread in a little olive oil, season generously and bake in a preheated oven at 180°C (350°F), Gas mark 4 for 8-10 minutes until crisp and golden brown, tossing occasionally to ensure they cook evenly.

Wine match
Australian Riesling
The pear flavours in the Australian Riesling will lift the flavour of the walnuts and pear.

Customer recipe — **Cathy Fennelly,**
Superquinn Portlaoise

chick
LITE

Chicken and mozzarella parcels

"This is one of my favourite ways of cooking chicken and it is great for entertaining. The parcels can be made up to 24 hours in advance and left covered with cling film in the fridge leaving very little to do last minute."

Serves 6

120 ml (4 fl oz) olive oil

1 fresh rosemary sprig

1 small garlic bulb, separated into cloves and peeled

6 large skinless chicken breast fillets

100 g ball mozzarella, cut into 6 slices

12 slices Parma ham (about 150 g (5 oz) in total)

Maldon sea salt and freshly ground black pepper

steamed long stemmed broccoli and crispy sautéed potatoes, to serve

To download the shopping list:
www.superquinn.ie/content/ChickenAnd
MozzarellaParcels/933

1   Place the olive oil in a small pan with the rosemary and garlic. Place on the lowest heat and cook very gently for 8–10 minutes until the garlic is soft and lightly golden. Transfer the garlic to a plate, discard the rosemary and reserve the oil. When the garlic has cooled cut into slices.

2   Preheat the oven to 180°C (350°F), Gas mark 4. Using a sharp knife, slit each chicken breast to make a pocket by cutting horizontally almost all the way through but leaving them attached at one side. Season to taste. Fill each one with a slice of mozzarella and divide the garlic slices among them, then give the filling a good grinding of black pepper and wrap in two slices of Parma ham to secure the filling.

3   Heat a little of the reserved oil in a frying pan and sauté the chicken fillets in batches for 1–2 minutes on each side until lightly golden. Arrange side-by-side in a baking dish and drizzle over the remaining oil. Bake for 15–20 minutes or until the chicken is cooked through and the Parma ham is crispy. Arrange on warmed plates with the broccoli and some sautéed potatoes to serve.

Wine match
Italian Pinot Grigio
A refreshing light white wine like a Pinot Grigio really sets off the Parma ham in this dish.

CATHY is a keen cook and shops in Superquinn Portlaoise for the excellent range of produce they have to offer.

flan TASTIC

This flan is delicious hot or cold. It is perfect for using up leftover ham or bacon from a joint, otherwise a packet of streaky bacon rashers, snipped into small pieces will do the trick, just lightly sauté them first. If you haven't got the correct flan tin use a similar sized small baking dish or roasting tin, which will do the job just as well.

Blue cheese, bacon and spinach flan

Serves 4

50 g (2 oz) butter, plus extra for greasing

1 small onion, finely chopped

350 g (12 oz) fresh spinach, washed and large stalks removed

5 sheets filo pastry, thawed

100 g (4 oz) cooked ham or loin of bacon, cut into cubes

75 g (3 oz) blue cheese (such as Crozier blue, Cashel Blue or Bellingham Blue)

3 eggs

6 tbsp crème fraîche

salt and freshly ground black pepper

lightly dressed green salad and boiled new potatoes, to serve

To download the shopping list:
www.superquinn.ie/content/BlueCheese
BaconAndSpinachFlan/934

1 Preheat the oven to 180°C (350°F), Gas mark 4. Lightly butter a 35 x 11 cm (14 x 4 ½ in) loose-bottomed flan tin. Heat a large non-stick frying pan. Add a knob of the butter and sauté the onion for 4–5 minutes until softened but not coloured. Stir in the spinach and cook for a few minutes until wilted, stirring. Turn the mixture into a sieve and press well with a wooden spoon to squeeze out all of the excess liquid.

2 Melt the butter in a small pan or in the microwave. Lay one sheet of filo across the base of the tin with the edges slightly overhanging the sides. Brush with melted butter. Repeat with the remaining sheets, arranging them at different, overlapping angles.

3 Spoon the spinach and onion mixture into the pastry case and scatter the ham or bacon on top, then crumble over the blue cheese. Beat together the eggs, crème fraîche and seasoning in a bowl, then pour over into the pastry case. Bake for 30 minutes until the filling is just set and the filo pastry is golden. Serve cut into slices and arrange on plates with salad and new potatoes.

Wine match
Côtes du Rhône
The lightness Côtes du Rhône works very well to compliment bacon and spinach and the strong blue cheese.

Irish BRED

This is an Irish version of a great British classic that is extremely versatile. To make them into more of a meal, add some hand-carved roast ham (page 102) and serve with a lightly dressed rocket salad on the side.

Irish rarebit with vine-ripened tomatoes on batch bread

Serves 4-6

225 g (8 oz) vintage Cheddar cheese, grated

3 eggs

1 tsp prepared English mustard

few drops of Worcestershire sauce

4 thick slices batch white bread

2 vine-ripened tomatoes, sliced

Maldon sea salt and freshly ground black pepper

To download the shopping list:
www.superquinn.ie/content/IrishRarebit
WithVineRipenedTomatoesOnBatch/935

1 Preheat the oven to 220°C (425°F), Gas mark 7. Place the Cheddar in a bowl. Separate the eggs and add the yolks to the Cheddar with the mustard and Worcestershire sauce. Season to taste. Place the egg whites in a separate bowl.

2 Whisk the egg whites with an electric mixer until they stand in stiff peaks. Add a spoonful of the beaten egg whites into the cheese mixture, then gently fold the rest of the egg whites.

3 Lightly toast the slices of white bread in a toaster. Arrange on a baking sheet, then add the tomatoes in a slightly overlapping layer. Spoon over the rarebit mixture and bake for 8–10 minutes until risen and lightly browned. Transfer on to plates, then cut in half on the diagonal to serve.

Wine match
Amarone della Valpolicella
The Amarone works perfectly with the juicy tomatoes and is powerful enough to match the heat of the mustard and the strong flavour of the cheese.

DEVIL.
mint

This is a wonderful salad to serve with lamb, whether you cook it on the barbecue or a griddle pan. Of course, nectarines also work well depending on what is available.

Feta cheese salad with griddled peaches and mint

Serves 4

2 tbsp olive oil

4 ripe firm peaches, stoned and cut into wedges

juice of 1 lime

200 g (7 oz) bag watercress, spinach and rocket salad leaves

1 small red onion, thinly sliced

small handful fresh mint leaves

200 g (7 oz) feta cheese, roughly crumbled

freshly ground black pepper

To download the shopping list:
www.superquinn.ie/content/FetaCheeseSalad
WithGriddledPeachesAndMint/936

1 Heat a cast-iron ridged griddle pan until smoking hot, then brush with half of the oil. Toss the peaches in half of the lime juice and place flesh-side down on to the griddle and cook for 2–3 minutes until lightly charred, turning once.

2 Place the remaining oil in a large bowl with the rest of the lime juice, the salad leaves and red onion. Roughly tear the mint and scatter on top, then divide among plates.

3 Scatter the charred peaches over the dressed salad mixture and crumble the feta cheese on top. Season with pepper and serve immediately.

Wine match
Viognier
The Viognier has plenty of fruit and acidity to work with the sweetness of the peach and the saltiness of the feta.

board MEETING

The ultimate cheeseboard with fig chutney

For any cheese lover, the idea of being able to work your way around a selection of contrasting cheeses is one of the best ways of indulging your passion. When putting together a cheeseboard the aim is for a contrast of textures, tastes and shapes. Mild to strong, rounds and wedges, light against dark, soft and hard – it's about making an aesthetic impact as much as a gastrominoc one. The chutney will keep in the fridge for up to two weeks.

Serves 4-6

350 g (12 oz) wedge Ardrahan cheese (washed-rind semi-soft cheese)

200 g packet Cooleeney (soft molded creamy cheese)

190 g carton Ardsallagh soft goat's cheese

275 g (10 oz) wedge Coolea farmhouse Gouda

250 g (9 oz) wedge mature Bellingham Blue (unpasteurised)

For the fig chutney:

2 tbsp olive oil

2 red onions, thinly sliced

1 small Bramley apple, peeled, cored and finely chopped

150 g (5 oz) ready-to-eat dried figs, finely chopped

2 tbsp balsamic vinegar

100 ml (3 ½ fl oz) ruby red port

2 tbsp light muscovado sugar

1 tsp chopped fresh thyme

Maldon sea salt and freshly ground black pepper

selection different types of crackers and seedless red grapes, to serve

To download the shopping list:
www.superquinn.ie/content/TheUltimate
CheeseboardWithFigChutney/937

1 To make the chutney, heat the olive oil in a large pan and tip in the red onions, then sauté for 10 minutes until softened, stirring occasionally. Stir in apple, figs, balsamic vinegar, port, sugar and thyme until well combined. Cook for about 10 minutes until slightly reduced and thickened, stirring occasionally. Season to taste. Blend in a food processor for 1–2 minutes until smooth, then leave to cool completely. Store in an airtight container and use as required.

2 At least a half an hour before you are ready to serve, remove all the cheeses from the fridge and their packaging. Arrange on a wooden board with a bowl of the fig chutney and a selection of crackers and small mounds of the grapes. Hand around plates to each guest and allow people to help themselves.

Chef's top tip –

Ideally the ultimate cheeseboard should contain a cheese from one of each of the main styles (see suggestions above). However, you can also just serve one hero cheese in perfect condition with excellent impact. It can also be a good idea to introduce a cheese that many of your guests have never tried before.

Wine match
St. Émilion Grand Cru
The St. Émilion is the perfect partner for this mix of cheese and the fruitiness of the fig chutney.

critical PANNING

This is a variation on the traditional way of cooking potatoes in a cast-iron frying pan over an open fire. They're delicious on their own with just a salad, or try serving simply with grilled fish or a steak.

Irish stoved potatoes with vintage Cheddar

Serves 4-6

675 g (1 ½ lb) potatoes

knob of butter

1 tbsp olive oil

2 onions, thinly sliced

100 g (4 oz) vintage Cheddar cheese, grated

Maldon sea salt and freshly ground white pepper

 To download the shopping list:
www.superquinn.ie/content/IrishStoved PotatoesWithVintageCheddar/938

1 Peel the potatoes and slice thinly on a Japanese mandolin or with a very sharp knife.

2 Heat the butter and oil in a heavy-based frying pan that is about 20 cm (8 in) in diameter and about 5 cm (2 in) deep. Remove from the heat and cover the base with a layer of the potatoes.

3 Add a layer of onions over the potatoes and another of grated cheese, seasoning generously as you go. Continue these layers, finishing with a layer of potatoes and a sprinkling of cheese.

4 Cover tightly with tin foil and cook over a very low heat for 45 minutes to 1 hour until potatoes on top are just cooked through when pierced with a sharp knife.

5 Preheat the grill. Uncover the stoved potatoes and place straight under the grill for 2–3 minutes to brown. Serve straight from the pan.

Chef's top tip —

Choose firm–fleshed potatoes for this recipe such as Roosters or Maris Piper as they will keep their shape during cooking and don't break up. Of course, this recipe could also be baked in the oven if you'd prefer.

doubling UP

This is a fabulously rich cheese soufflé that gets baked twice. It really couldn't be simpler to make and you don't have any last minute worries about whether they're going to rise.

Twice baked cheese soufflé

Serves 4

40 g (1 ½ oz) butter, plus extra for greasing

50 g (2 oz) plain flour

250 ml (8 fl oz) milk

4 eggs, separated

1 tbsp snipped fresh chives

2 tbsp freshly grated Parmesan

3 tbsp cream

75 g (3 oz) Comté cheese, grated (unpasteurised)

Maldon sea salt and freshly ground black pepper

To download the shopping list:
www.superquinn.ie/content/TwiceBaked
CheeseSouffle/939

Chef's top tip —

These soufflés can be kept warm at 130°C (250°F), Gas mark ½ for up to 30 minutes, but no longer as they start to dry out and go rubbery.

1 Preheat the oven to 190°C (375°F), Gas mark 5. Melt the butter in a pan. Remove from the heat and beat in the flour until smooth. Return to the heat, add the milk and whisk to form a smooth sauce. Once the sauce has thickened, remove from the heat and leave to cool for a few minutes.

2 Add the egg yolks to the cooled sauce with the chives and a little seasoning and beat thoroughly to combine. Place the egg whites in a separate bowl and beat until soft peaks have formed, then carefully fold into the sauce mixture.

3 Grease 4 x 200ml (7 fl oz) ramekins and dust with the Parmesan, knocking out any excess. Pour the mixture into the prepared ramekins and bake for 20–25 minutes. Once they are done, leave for a couple of minutes in the ramekins and then carefully take them out and leave on a baking sheet. (At this point you could leave them in the fridge, once completely cool, for a day or so if covered in cling film; or you could freeze them too).

4 When you are ready to bake the soufflés for a second time, preheat the oven to 160°C (325°F), Gas mark 3. Mix together the cream with the Comté cheese, then season to taste. Carefully make a small well in the top of each soufflé and spoon in the cheese mixture. Pop into the oven for at least 10 minutes until the cheese has melted and the soufflés have puffed up and risen again. Transfer to warmed plates with a metal fish slice and spoon any resulting sauce on top to serve.

Wine match
Sparkling Red
The lightness of the soufflé really calls for bubbles whilst the red fruit works well with the cheese

the BUTCHERY
choice
CUTS

THE BUTCHERY

W hat would Sunday be without a roast? When family and friends gather – there is nothing more certain to draw them in than the smell of a roast wafting its herby, garlicky way through the kitchen. To create the perfect roast dinner you don't need much, just good company and great quality meat.

Excellent meat is something that Ireland is famous for, and that is why, at Superquinn, 100% of the fresh meat and poultry sold in-store is Irish and fully traceable back to the farm of origin. Once you can be sure of the quality of your meat – you can get on with enjoying the myriad ways of serving it. Like roast rib of beef, seared almost black on the outside and meltingly pink in the middle or lemon, garlic and rosemary-infused chicken.

And, of course, what about the simple pleasure of a weekday supper of sausages with garlic mash and caramelised onion gravy or some super-succulent honey roast duck breasts served with Asian greens.

pie CHART

These pies can be made up to 24 hours in advance and kept in the fridge, ready to bake. They are delicious served with any crisp green vegetable.

Beef, mushroom and stout pie

Serves 6

4 tbsp sunflower oil

1 kg (2 ¼ lb) round steak, well trimmed and cut into cubes

2 onions, finely chopped

4 carrots, finely sliced

4 celery sticks, finely chopped

600ml (1 pint) stout

1 litre (1 ¾ pints) beef or chicken stock

250 g (9 oz) flat breakfast mushrooms, stems removed and chopped

600 g (1 lb 6 oz) self-raising flour, plus extra for dusting

300 g (11 oz) shredded vegetable suet

Maldon sea salt and freshly ground black pepper

To download the shopping list:
www.superquinn.ie/content/BeefMushroom
AndStoutPie/940

Wine match
Red Bordeaux
This dish needs a firm, dry red with body to set off the full flavour of the beef.

1 Heat one tablespoon of the oil in a large pan with a lid. Sauté half of the beef until well coloured. Transfer to a plate and repeat until all the beef is cooked.

2 Add the rest of the oil to the pan and sauté the onions, carrots and celery for 10 minutes without colouring. Pour in the stout and simmer gently to reduce by half, scraping the bottom of the pan to remove any sediment. Return the beef to the pan with the stout stock and mushrooms, then season, cover and simmer over the gentlest heat for 1–1 ½ hours until the beef is just tender but still holding its shape. Strain through a colander set over a bowl to cool, reserving the liquid.

3 Preheat the oven to 220°C (425°F), Gas mark 7. To make the pastry crust, sieve the flour into a bowl, stir in the suet and add just enough cold water to make a firm dough – 400 ml (14 fl oz) is about right. Rest for 5 minutes, then cut into six pieces and roll out each one on a lightly floured board to a circle that is about 1cm (½ in) thick.

4 Divide the meat among individual pie dishes that hold about 450 ml (¾ pint) and pour over enough of the gravy to come almost to the top. Do not overfill. Cut off the superfluous strip of each pastry circle, dampen the rim of each dish and press the pastry strip firmly into place around the rim. Dampen the pastry strip in turn and lay the pastry lids on top. Press down to fit the lid and then press all around with a fork dipped in water to seal the edges. Prick the tops with a fork and then transfer to baking sheets. Bake for 30–40 minutes until the pastry is puffed up and golden brown. Serve set on plates and straight to the table.

crowd PLEASER

A rib of beef is an excellent cut for roasting and perfect when you've got to feed a crowd. Always allow a joint to come back up to room temperature before roasting to achieve the best flavour.

Roast rib of beef on the bone with crispy, garlic roast potatoes

Serves 6–8

1.75 kg (4 lb) rib of beef on the bone

1 tsp black peppercorns

2 tsp Maldon sea salt

¼ tsp English mustard powder

1.5 kg (3 lb) even-sized potatoes, peeled

4 tbsp olive oil

1 garlic bulb, broken into cloves (not peeled)

1 tsp fresh mixed thyme and rosemary

1 large onion, roughly chopped

1 large carrot, roughly chopped

2 tsp plain flour

300 ml (½ pint) beef or chicken stock

creamed horseradish, to serve

Wine match
St. Émilion
The deep flavours of this dish call for a full bodied red like the St. Émilion.

To download the shopping list:
www.superquinn.ie/content/RoastRibOfBeef
OnTheBoneWithCrispyGarlicRoastPotatoes/941

1 Preheat the oven to 230°C (450°F), Gas mark 8. Heat a small frying pan and toast the peppercorns until aromatic, then place in a pestle and mortar and grind until cracked. Mix in half the salt and the mustard powder. Wipe the meat with damp kitchen paper and then lightly criss-cross the fat with a sharp knife. Rub with the peppercorn mixture.

2 Place the potatoes in a pan of salted water and bring to the boil. Simmer for 2–3 minutes, then drain and return to the pan. Toss vigorously to knock off the sharp edges and then drizzle in half the olive oil and add the garlic cloves and herbs. Toss again until evenly coated.

3 Pour the rest of the olive oil into roasting tin and add the onion and carrot, tossing to coat. Season to taste and sit the beef on the bed of vegetables. Arrange the potatoes and garlic cloves around the joint and season with the rest of the salt. Roast for 15 minutes and then reduce the oven temperature to 200°C (400°F), Gas mark 6 and roast for 10 minutes per 450 g (1 lb) for rare; 12 minutes for medium-rare and 20–25 minutes for well done. Take out and baste halfway through the cooking and quickly turn over the roast potatoes. A joint this size should take just under an hour.

4 Remove the beef from the tin and place on a platter to rest for 15 minutes before carving. Pop the potatoes back into a roasting tin and continue to cook in the oven. To make the gravy, stir the flour into the juices in the roasting tin and then gradually stir in the stock. Place directly on the hob to heat and simmer for 5 minutes, stirring with a wooden spoon. Pour through a sieve into a gravy boat. To serve, carve the beef into slices and arrange on warmed plates with a dollop of horseradish and the roasted potatoes. Hand round the gravy separately.

CUSTOMER RECIPE — ANN CARROLL,
SUPERQUINN SUTTON

rib TICKLER

Sticky baked ribs

"This recipe has taken me years to perfect. These ribs are slow-roasted until meltingly tender and then finished off in a hotter oven. Of course they can also be finished on the barbecue with great success."

Serves 4

4 tbsp clear honey

3 tbsp light muscovado sugar

1 tbsp Worcestershire sauce

2 tbsp tomato ketchup

1 tbsp red wine vinegar

1.5 kg (3 lb) pork ribs, chopped in half (each one should be roughly 7.5 cm (3 in)

salt and freshly ground black pepper

 To download the shopping list:
www.superquinn.ie/content/StickyBaked Ribs/942

Wine match
Alsace Riesling
The sweetness of this dish requires a suitably sweet wine like an Alsace Riesling.

1 Preheat the oven to 160°C (325°F), Gas mark 3. Place the honey in a small pan with the muscovado sugar, Worcestershire sauce, tomato ketchup, mustard, vinegar and season to taste. Heat gently until just simmering, stirring to dissolve the sugar. Remove from the heat and allow to cool.

2 Place the ribs in a large roasting tin and pour over the cooled sauce, tossing to coat. Cover tightly with foil and roast for 1 ¼ hours until the ribs are meltingly tender, turning and basting the ribs every so often and skimming off any excess fat.

3 Remove the foil from the ribs and drain off the excess sauce into a pan. Skim off any fat and reduce down until thickened, stirring occasionally. Increase the oven temperature to 200°C (400°F), Gas mark 6. Return the ribs to the oven for 10–15 minutes until nicely glazed, brushing a little of the reduced down sauce.

4 Arrange the ribs on a warmed platter to serve and put the rest of the sauce in a dish to the side. Have plenty of napkins and finger bowls of water for guests to have to hand.

Chef's top tip —

Ask at the butcher counter for nice meaty pork ribs and get them to chop them into 7.5cm (3 in) pieces, it saves you the job. Alternatively do this yourself using a heavy, sharp cleaver that can cut through bones.

ANN, the overall winner of the Superquinn recipe competition, is a big fan of Super Scan since her six-year-old granddaughter introduced her to it. A frequent shopper at Superquinn Sutton she finds it a very efficient way to shop and beat the queues.

WARMreception

> This is a great dish when you've got people to feed but want to enjoy the company. It can be made up to two days in advance and the added bonus is that the flavour just continues to improve.

Braised venison with smoked bacon and button mushrooms

Serves 4–6

2 tbsp olive oil

500 g packet venison haunch roast

2 carrots, cut into chunks

1 large onion, roughly chopped

2 garlic cloves, crushed

600 ml (1 pint) red wine

1.2 litres (2 pints) beef stock

2 each fresh thyme and rosemary sprigs

1 tbsp Dijon mustard

3 tbsp redcurrant jelly

150 g (5 oz) piece smoked bacon, rind removed and diced

150 g (5 oz) button mushrooms, wiped

Maldon sea salt and freshly ground white pepper

chopped fresh flat-leaf parsley, to garnish

creamy mashed potato, to serve

Wine match
Barolo
The strong flavour of this dish allows for a rich full bodied wine like the Italian Barolo.

 To download the shopping list:
www.superquinn.ie/content/BraisedVenison
WithSmokedBaconAndButtonMushrooms/943

1 Preheat oven to 160°C (325°F), Gas mark 3. Heat one tablespoon of the oil in a large casserole dish with a lid. Add the venison haunch and quickly sauté on all sides until browned. Transfer to a plate and set aside.

2 Add another tablespoon of oil to the casserole, reduce the heat a little and add the carrots, onion and garlic. Cook for a further 5 minutes until golden brown, stirring. Pour in the red wine, stirring to remove any sediment from the bottom.

3 Return the venison haunch to the casserole and pour over the beef stock. Add the herbs, mustard and redcurrant jelly and then season to taste. Cover tightly with foil and a lid and bake for 1 ½ hours until the venison is meltingly tender. Remove the venison from the braising juices and leave to rest on a warmed plate covered with foil. Strain the cooking juices into a pan and reduce down on a rapid simmer until well reduced and thickened. Carve or shred the venison.

4 Meanwhile, reheat the large non-stick frying pan. Add the remaining oil and sauté the bacon and mushrooms for 4–5 minutes until golden brown. Drain off oil and stir into the reduced down braising juices. Season to taste.

5 Place some mash in each wide-rimmed warmed bowl and place the venison on top. Ladle over the braising juice and garnish with parsley to serve.

FIRST crush

This is a twist on a traditional dish with a fantastic brioche crust. All of the juices from the lamb soak into the vegetables to make them even more delicious than usual. The root vegetables finish cooking as the lamb is resting so everything is ready to serve at the same time.

Brioche crushed rack of lamb with roasted root vegetables

Serves 4–6

200 g (7 oz) brioche bread (slightly stale is fine)

2 tbsp chopped fresh flat-leaf parsley

1 tsp each fresh thyme and rosemary leaves

1 large garlic clove, chopped

100 g (4 oz) butter

2 racks of lamb, well trimmed (each about 675 g (1 ½ lb)

2 tbsp Dijon mustard

For the roasted root vegetables:

2 tbsp olive oil

1 kg (2 ¼ lb) mixed root vegetables, trimmed and even-sized cut into chunks (such as carrots, parsnips, swede and / or sweet potatoes)

1 tbsp clear honey

Maldon sea salt and freshly ground black pepper

Wine match
Rioja Reserva
The hint of mint in the Rioja is simply stunning with lamb.

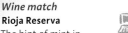 **To download the shopping list:**
www.superquinn.ie/content/BriocheCrushed RackOfLambWithRoastedRootVegetables/944

1 Break the brioche into large pieces and place in a food processor and blitz into fine crumbs. Add the herbs and garlic and blend again briefly. Melt the butter in a small pan or in the microwave, then fold into the crumbs and season to taste.

2 Place the racks of lamb on a chopping board and using a pastry brush, spread the mustard thickly over the fat side of each rack. Cover with the brioche crust, using your hands to mould it over the lamb. Arrange the lamb, coated-side up in a baking sheet and chill for at least 30 minutes; up to two hours is fine to allow the crust to 'set'.

3 Preheat the oven to 200°C (400°F), Gas mark 6. Place the oil in a large roasting tin and add the root vegetables. Toss everything together until well coated and season generously. Arrange the racks of lamb on top and roast for 20 minutes per 450 g (1 lb) for pink lamb; longer if you prefer your meat more well done.

4 Transfer the racks of lamb to a plate and leave to rest in a warm place, then drizzle the honey over the root vegetables and then give them a good toss and cook for another 10–15 minutes or until the vegetables are just beginning to catch and caramelise around the edges. Carve the racks of lamb into chops and arrange on a warmed platter with the roasted root vegetables. Serve straight to the table.

GOLD plated

This recipe takes some pork fillet and makes it into something really special. It takes a bit of planning, as the prunes need to be soaked for at least an hour. If you have time, leaving them to soak overnight is best to plump them up and making the extra effort is well worth it.

Pan-fried medallions of pork with prunes

Serves 4

150 ml (¼ pint) dry white wine

12 ready-to-eat prunes

450 g (1 lb) tenderloin pork fillet

1 tbsp seasoned flour

25 g (1 oz) butter

1 tbsp redcurrant jelly

150 ml (¼ pint) cream

squeeze of lemon juice

salt and freshly ground black pepper

French green beans, to serve

To download the shopping list:
www.superquinn.ie/content/PanFried
MedallionsOfPorkWithPrunes/945

Chef's top tip –

This would also be delicious served with a celeriac and potato puree. Simply boil equal quantities of the vegetables until tender and then mash with a good knob of butter and a splash of milk. Season to taste before serving.

1. Place the white wine and prunes in a bowl and set aside for at least 1 hour to soak (preferably overnight).

2. Trim the pork and cut into 12 even-sized medallions. Season well and dust in the flour, shaking off any excess.

3. Heat the butter in a large sauté pan until foaming and cook the pork medallions in two batches for 1–2 minutes on each side. Transfer to a plate and set aside.

4. Strain the wine into the hot pan and bring to the boil. Stir in the redcurrant jelly and cook for a further 2 minutes, stirring until syrupy. Add the cream, prunes and pork; season to taste and simmer gently for 3–4 minutes or until the pork is just tender and cooked through. Add the lemon juice to taste and season to taste. Arrange on warmed plates with some French green beans.

Wine match
Fleurie
The fruitiness of the medium bodied Fleurie accentuates the prunes beautifully in this dish.

ham it UP

This ham is perfect if you've got a crowd to feed for any celebration or over the festive period. It tastes equally good served hot or cold.

Baked ham glazed with orange marmalade

Serves 10–12

3 kg (6 lb) ham fillet

4 celery sticks, roughly chopped

2 onions, sliced

1 bunch fresh thyme

1 tablespoon black peppercorns

2 oranges

6 tbsp orange marmalade (from a jar)

freshly ground black pepper

braised red cabbage with pomegranate (page 49) and jacket potatoes topped with soured cream & chives, to serve

To download the shopping list:
www.superquinn.ie/content/BakedHam
GlazedWithOrangeMarmalade/946

1. Place the ham in a large but snug-fitting pan. Cover it with water, then add the celery, onions, thyme and peppercorns. Peel the rind from the oranges and add to the water and then squeeze in the juice. Bring to the boil, then turn the heat down and simmer for an hour and a quarter with a lid on, skimming as necessary. Remove from the heat and allow to cool for half an hour in the broth. This will allow the flavours to really penetrate the meat.

2. Preheat the oven to 160°C (325°F), Gas mark 3. Transfer the ham to a board and, using a knife, carefully take off the skin, leaving the string holding the joint together intact. Remove some of the fat as well, to leave you with about 1 cm (½ in). Score the fat left on the ham in a criss-cross fashion, and while it's moist, season generously with pepper. Place in a roasting tin and roast for 20 minutes until the fat renders and becomes slightly crispy.

3. Strain the vegetables from the broth and reserve 300 ml (½ pint). The remainder can be used for making minestrone-type soups – it will freeze for use another day. Remove the ham from the oven and smear over the marmalade, then pour in the reserved broth to help keep the joint moist and prevent the marmalade from sticking to the tin and burning.

4. Return the ham to the oven and roast for another hour (or according to instructions depending on the size of your joint) until beautifully golden and crisp. Cover loosely with foil and leave to rest for about 30 minutes before carving and arranging on plates with the braised red cabbage and jacket potatoes to serve.

Wine match
Beaujolais Villages
A medium bodied red like the Beaujolais Villages is the perfect partner here so as not to overpower the ham.

BERRY Christmas

To be confident that the turkey is cooked through invest in a meat thermometer and push it into the thickest part of one of the thighs. This will then clearly show you when the turkey is ready leaving no doubt in your mind.

Roast turkey with cranberry sausage stuffing

Serves 10–12

6 kg (12 lb) oven-ready whole turkey, at room temperature

100 g (4 oz) butter, at room temperature

1 tbsp plain flour

600 ml (1 pint) chicken stock

For the cranberry sausage stuffing:

50 g (2 oz) butter

1 large onion, finely chopped

2 celery sticks, finely chopped

175 g (6 oz) fresh white breadcrumbs

2 tbsp chopped fresh mixed herbs (such as parsley, sage and thyme)

225 g (8 oz) sausage meat

100 g (4 oz) fresh cranberries

salt and freshly ground black pepper

roast potatoes and baked carrot batons in a bag with thyme (see page 43)

 To download the shopping list:
www.superquinn.ie/content/RoastTurkey
WithCranberrySausageStuffing/947

Wine match
Chablis Premier Cru
Roast Turkey is usually reserved for Christmas so why not indulge a little during the festive season with a beautiful Chablis Premier Cru.

1 Preheat the oven to 190°C (375°F), Gas mark 5. To make the stuffing, melt the butter in a frying pan and sauté the onion and celery for 5 minutes until softened. Mix in the breadcrumbs, herbs, sausage meat and cranberries, then season to taste. Pack inside the turkey neck and secure with a small skewer or a scrunched up piece of foil.

2 Smear the skin of the turkey all over with some of the butter and season. Turn the turkey breast-side up and tie the top of the drumsticks with string. Weigh the turkey to calculate the required cooking time, allowing 20 minutes per 450 g (1 lb) plus 20 minutes – this size should take about 4 hours and 20 minutes.

3 Lay a large sheet of foil lengthways over a large roasting tin, leaving enough at each end to wrap over the turkey, then lightly butter the foil. Repeat this exercise with another sheet of foil, this time across the tin. Lightly butter once again. Place the stuffed turkey breast-side up in the centre of the foil, then wrap loosely to enclose, allowing air to circulate around the turkey.

4 Place in the oven and cook according the calculated cooking time, unwrapping and basting every 40 minutes. For the final hour, fold back and remove the foil, then baste well and return to the oven. To check its cooked, insert a fine skewer into the thickest part of the thigh: the juices should run clear, but if they are still pink, return to the oven and check every 15 minutes until the turkey is cooked right the way through. Remove from the oven and transfer to a warmed platter. Cover with foil and leave to rest in a warm place for about 20 minutes.

5 Place the roasting tin directly on the hob over a gentle heat and skim any excess fat from the cooking juices. Stir the flour into the tin's residue. Cook on the hob for a minute or two, stirring until golden. Gradually add the stock, stirring until smooth after each addition. Bring to the boil and let it bubble for 10 minutes until reduced and thickened, stirring occasionally. Season to taste.

6 Bring the turkey to the table, then carve into slices and arrange on warmed plates with some of the gravy, the roast potatoes, baked carrot batons (see page 43), and stuffing to serve.

STEAKS
are high

Here's an idea for something a little bit different the next time you fancy a steak. This steak with melting Cashel Blue butter is so delicious that it's hard to believe how little time it takes to prepare, just a little bit of forward planning to allow time for the flavoured butter to firm up in the fridge.

Griddled ribeye with Cashel Blue butter and roasted cherry tomatoes

Serves 4

50 g (2 oz) unsalted butter, softened

50 g (2 oz) Cashel Blue cheese

1 tbsp snipped fresh chives

450 g (1 lb) Oilean potatoes, scraped or scrubbed clean

4 tbsp olive oil

pinch of chopped fresh thyme

4 cherry tomato vines, each with 5–7 tomatoes

4 x 225 g (8 oz) ribeye dry aged steaks

Maldon sea salt and freshly ground black pepper

To download the shopping list:
www.superquinn.ie/content/GriddledRibeyeWith
CashelBlueButterAndRoastedCherryTomatoes/948

Wine match
Chateauneuf-du-Pape
The style of this dish calls for a more full bodied wine with more tannic like the Chateauneuf-du-Pape.

1 Mash the butter and Cashel blue cheese in a bowl with a fork until just combined. Stir in the chives and season to taste. Using a white spatula, transfer on to a sheet of parchment paper, then shape into a roll about 4 cm (1 ½ in) thick and wrap up tightly. Chill for at least 1 hour until firm.

2 Preheat the oven to 200°C (400°F), Gas mark 6. Cut the potatoes into 5 mm (¼ in) slices and arrange in a single layer in a roasting tin lined with non-stick parchment paper. Add two tablespoons of the olive oil, the thyme and season with salt, then toss to coat. Arrange the cherry tomato vines around the edges of the roasting tin and drizzle over another tablespoon of the olive oil, then season with salt. Roast for 15–20 minutes until tender and lightly golden.

3 Heat a griddle pan until smoking hot. Rub the steaks with olive oil and season generously with black pepper. Cook for 4–6 minutes on each side, if you like your beef rare – a little longer if you don't. Cut the Cashel Blue butter into slices. Remove the steaks from the heat and transfer to warmed plates. Top with the slices of butter and leave to rest for about 5 minutes in a warm place. Add the rustic roasted tray potatoes to the rested steaks with melting Cashel Blue butter. Arrange a vine of roasted cherry tomatoes on each plate to serve.

Chef's top tip –

It is worth investing in a good quality cast iron ridged griddle pan. They need no looking after and ensure perfect results every time. If the steak is still sticking to the ridges, then leave it alone until the meat contracts back from the pan.

true
PORKIES

This gravy takes a little while to make but it is well worth the effort. If you think you're going to be short of time you can make it well in advance and heat it through at the last minute. Otherwise, make a double batch when you do go to the trouble as it freezes very well.

Sausages with garlic mash and caramelised onion gravy

Serves 4

25 g (1 oz) butter

450 g (1 lb) red onions, halved and thinly sliced

½ tsp sugar

good splash of red wine

1 tbsp plain flour

300 ml (½ pint) beef stock

1 tbsp sunflower oil

12 pork sausages

For the garlic mash:

900 g (2 lb) potatoes, cut into chunks

6 tbsp milk

2 garlic cloves, peeled

25 g (1 oz) butter

Maldon sea salt and freshly ground black pepper

chopped fresh flat-leaf parsley, to garnish

Wine match
Fitou
Fitou is a great flavoursome wine to compliment the richness of the gravy and sausage.

To download the shopping list:
www.superquinn.ie/content/SausagesWithGarlicMash
AndCaramelisedOnionGravy/949

1 To make the gravy, melt half the butter in a large frying pan and add the onions and sugar, then cook over a medium heat for 20–30 minutes until caramelised, stirring occasionally. Pour in the wine and allow to bubble down and then simmer until it has almost disappeared. Stir in the flour and cook for 1 minute, stirring. Gradually add the stock, then season to taste and simmer gently until you have achieved a rich gravy. Keep warm.

2 To make the garlic mash, place the potatoes in a covered pan of boiling water and simmer for 15–20 minutes until tender. After about 10 minutes, heat the oil in a large frying pan and cook the sausages for about 10 minutes until golden brown, turning regularly. Place the milk in a small pan with the garlic and simmer gently until the garlic is completely soft, then mash down with a fork.

3 Drain the potatoes and mash until smooth, then beat in the butter with the milk and garlic mixture. Season to taste. Divide the mash among warmed plates and arrange the sausages alongside. Spoon over the caramelised onion gravy and garnish with the parsley to serve.

CUSTOMER RECIPE — ANDREA CRONNOLLY,
SUPERQUINN SUTTON

SWEET as

Honey roast duck breasts

"My husband Ed loves these duck breasts and the great thing is that there is no preparation involved – an important point with four young children in the house! I like to serve them slightly pink in the centre, but just cook them for a few minutes longer if you prefer them more well done."

ANDREA tends to pop into her local Superquinn Sutton on a daily basis. She values the freshness of the fruit and vegetables and always uses the meat counter for the personalised service.

Serves 4

4 x 175 g (6 oz) duck breasts

3 tbsp dark soy sauce

4 tsp clear honey

1 shallot, finely chopped

1 red chilli, seeded and finely chopped

stir-fried pak choy and fragrant steamed Thai rice, to serve

 To download the shopping list:
www.superquinn.ie/content/
HoneyRoastDuckBreasts/950

Wine match
Alsace Gewurtztraminer
The sweetness of this dish requires a suitably sweet wine like an Alsace Gewurtztraminer.

1 Trim down each duck breast and then lightly score the skin into a diamond pattern with the tip of a sharp knife, taking care not to cut through to the flesh.

2 Heat a large heavy-based frying pan (or you may need two depending on their size) until it is quite hot. Add the duck breasts, skin side down, lower the heat to medium and cook for about 3–4 minutes until the skin is crisp and golden brown.

3 Turn the breasts over and cook them for another 5 minutes, or a little longer if you don't like your duck too pink. Meanwhile, mix together the soy sauce, honey, shallot and chilli in a small bowl.

4 Pour away all of the excess fat from the pan. Add the soy sauce mixture and leave it to bubble away, turning the duck breasts occasionally for 1–2 minutes, until they are nicely glazed. Remove from the heat and leave to rest in a warm place for a couple of minutes.

5 Slice each duck breast on the diagonal and carefully transfer to warmed plates. Spoon over any remaining glaze. Add some stir-fried pak choy and rice to serve.

STAFF RECIPE — ÁINE DOWLING,
SUPERQUINN HEAD OFFICE

Thai & MIGHTY

Thai-style chicken with beansprouts

"For me this is a perfect mid week meal, as it should take you no more than fifteen minutes to prepare and get on the table. Use any selection of vegetables you fancy, depending on what is available. It is great served with noodles or steamed rice."

Serves 2 – 4

2 tbsp dark soy sauce

1 tbsp Thai fish sauce (nam pla)

1 tbsp clear honey

1 tsp light muscovado sugar

2 tbsp sunflower oil

2 shallots, thinly sliced

3 garlic cloves, thinly sliced

1 red chilli, seeded and finely chopped

2 large skinless chicken breast fillets, cut into bite-sized pieces

100 g (4 oz) thin green beans, trimmed and cut in half

50 g (2 oz) fresh beansprouts, trimmed

½ large lime

fresh coriander leaves, to garnish

medium egg noodles tossed in a little sesame oil, to serve

 To download the shopping list:
www.superquinn.ie/content/Thaistyle
ChickenWithBeansprouts/951

① Place the soy sauce in a small bowl and stir in the fish sauce, honey and sugar. Set aside until needed.

② Heat a wok until smoking hot. Add the sunflower oil and swirl up the sides, then tip in the shallots, garlic and chilli. Stir-fry for 1–2 minutes until sizzling.

③ Tip the chicken into the wok and continue to stir-fry for 2–3 minutes until sealed. Drizzle over the soy sauce mixture and cook for another minute or two until the chicken is nicely glazed.

④ Add the green beans to the chicken mixture, then squeeze over the lime juice and stir-fry for 2–3 minutes until the green beans still have a little bite, adding the beansprouts for the last 30 seconds or so to keep them crisp. Scatter over the coriander and arrange in warmed bowls with the noodles to serve.

Wine match
Australian Sauvignon-Semillion Blend
The fruit and breadth in this blend of wine compliments the Thai flavours of this dish perfectly.

ÁINE is the bakery buyer in Superquinn and has worked for Superquinn for over 4 years. This dish was inspired by her love of healthy fresh food and her need for quick meal solutions now that she is a successful working mum.

IN season

Roast chicken is a dinner that everyone in the family seems to enjoy and of course it makes the perfect Sunday lunch. The strong flavours of the lemon, rosemary and garlic here really penetrate the flesh of the chicken and give off the most wonderful aromas whilst cooking.

Roast chicken with lemon, rosemary and garlic

Serves 4

1.5 kg (3 lb) whole chicken

1 lemon

2 garlic bulbs

3 fresh rosemary sprigs

2 red onions, peeled and halved

8 small carrots, trimmed and peeled

3 tbsp olive oil

1 tbsp plain flour

450 ml (¾ pint) chicken stock

salt and freshly ground black pepper

crispy roast potatoes and garden peas, to serve

Wine match
Californian Chardonnay
This roast chicken is made really exciting with the lemon, butter and lightly oaked tones of a Californian Chardonnay.

To download the shopping list:
www.superquinn.ie/content/RoastChicken
WithLemonRosemaryAndGarlic/952

1 Take your chicken out of the fridge 30 minutes before it goes into the oven. Preheat the oven to 230°C (450°F), Gas mark 8. Cut the lemon and one of the garlic bulbs in half and place in the cavity of the chicken with the rosemary.

2 Separate the remaining garlic bulb into cloves and place in a roasting tin with the onions and carrots, tossing to coat in one tablespoon of the olive oil. Sit the chicken on top of the pile of vegetables and drizzle all over with the remaining olive oil, then season well, rubbing it all over. Place in the oven and then immediately reduce the heat to 200°C (400°F), Gas mark 6. Roast the chicken for 1 hour and 20 minutes, basting the chicken halfway through cooking.

3 When the chicken is cooked, transfer to a board and put the carrots and red onions on a warmed plate. Cover each with tin foil and leave to rest for 15 minutes while you make the gravy. Using a large spoon, carefully remove most of the fat from the tin and then place the tin directly on the heat. Stir in the flour and then pour in the stock, stirring continuously to blend the flour in. Bring to the boil, then reduce the heat and simmer for about 10 minutes until slightly reduced and thickened, stirring occasionally. Stir in the juices from the resting chicken and season to taste. Transfer to a warmed gravy boat.

4 Carve the chicken into slices and arrange on warmed plates with the reserved carrots and red onion halves and the crispy roast potatoes and garden peas. Pour over the gravy to serve.

just add FRIENDS

The secret to this dish is to use good quality sausages; choose from the fantastic selection now available, such as fresh venison or a more traditional pork & black pepper.

Sausage and bean cassoulet

Serves 4

25 g (1 oz) dried porcini mushrooms

3 tbsp olive oil

6 large honey & mustard pork sausages (400 g packet)

100 g (4 oz) pancetta (smoked streaky bacon lardons)

1 large onion, finely chopped

1 large carrot, diced

2 celery sticks, diced

1 garlic clove, finely chopped

1 tbsp chopped fresh sage

2 bay leaves

150 ml (¼ pint) red wine

400 g can chopped tomatoes

2 x 400 g cans cannellini beans, drained and rinsed

50 g (2 oz) fresh white breadcrumbs

Maldon sea salt and freshly ground black pepper

 To download the shopping list:
www.superquinn.ie/content/SausageAnd
BeanCassoulet/953

1. Preheat the oven to 180°C (350°F), Gas mark 4. Soak the porcini mushrooms in 500 ml (18 fl oz) of boiling water. Heat a casserole dish. Add a tablespoon of the olive oil and then add the sausages. Cook gently for 1–2 minutes or until just sealed and lightly browned on both sides. Transfer to a plate and set aside.

2. Add the rest of the olive oil to the casserole and sauté the pancetta until golden. Add the onion, carrot, celery, garlic and half of the sage and gently sauté for 8–10 minutes until softened.

3. Drain the porcini and roughly chop, then add to the casserole with the bay leaves. Sauté for another 2–3 minutes and then add the wine. Bring to the boil, then reduce the heat and simmer until reduced by half, scraping the bottom with a wooden spoon.

4. Pour in the reserved porcini liquid and tip in the tomatoes and beans. Season to taste and simmer for about 5 minutes until slightly reduced and thickened. Arrange the sausages on top, burying them down into the mixture. Mix the rest of the sage with the breadcrumbs and scatter on top. Roast for 25–30 until the cassoulet is bubbling and the sausages are cooked through and tender. Serve straight to the table and allow guests to help themselves.

Wine match
Corbières
This substantial dish can handle a big full bodied red like the Corbières from south-west France.

THE FISHMONGER
excellent
CATCH

THE FISHMONGER

F ast food is great. When you've had a long day and everyone's starving, the last thing you want to do is spend an hour preparing dinner. And that's when fresh fish really comes into its own. Not only is it nutritious and delicious but it also cooks in mere minutes.

With a fresh piece of fresh flat fish such as plaice or lemon sole all you have to do is dip in some tempura batter and deep-fry until crispy. With meatier round fish such as un-dyed smoked haddock, fresh cod or salmon – they work wonderfully well baked in a creamy fish pie in the oven. Or plump garlic mussels served with plenty of crusty bread to mop up all the delicious juices. Either way, in no time at all you could be enjoying a wonderful fish supper good enough to grace any smart restaurant table.

With twice daily deliveries and Bord Iascaigh Mhara's stamp of approval you can be sure you are getting the freshest and the best at Superquinn. And don't be afraid to ask questions at the counter, chances are the people behind you in the queue will be delighted you asked.

LIGHT
fantastic

These burgers need nothing to bind the salmon together except the wasabi. In fact this recipe would work well with any firm-fleshed fish such as tuna. Ask at the fish counter to ensure that all the skin and bones have been removed.

Wasabi salmon burgers with red onion salsa

Serves 4

550 g (1 ¼ lb) salmon fillet, skinned and boned

2 spring onions, thinly sliced

1 heaped tbsp wasabi paste

2 tsp sesame seeds

1 tbsp seasoned flour

3 tbsp olive oil

2 plum tomatoes, seeded and finely chopped

1 small red onion, finely diced

1 green chilli, seeded and finely chopped

juice of 1 lime, plus wedges to garnish

4 slices of rustic style bread

salt and freshly ground black pepper

little gem lettuce and fresh coriander sprigs, to serve

Wine match
New Zealand Pinot Noir
The spicy flavour of the wasabi and red onion salsa makes a soft, red such as the New Zealand Pinot Noir the perfect choice for this dish.

To download the shopping list:
www.www.superquinn.ie/content/WasabiSalmon
BurgersWithRedOnionSalsa/954

1   Using a large sharp knife, cut away any brown bits from the salmon fillet, then finely chop. Place in a bowl, then stir in the spring onions, wasabi paste and sesame seeds. Season to taste. Divide into four portions, then using slightly wetted hands, shape into patties. Dust in the flour, shaking off any excess.

2   Heat a large non-stick frying pan. Add two tablespoons of the oil to the frying pan and then add the salmon burgers. Cook for 2–3 minutes on each side until lightly golden but still slightly pink in the centre. Be careful not to overcook them or they'll quickly become dry.

3   Meanwhile, make the red onion salsa. Place the tomatoes in a bowl and stir in the red onion, chilli, lime juice and the rest of the olive oil.

4   Heat a griddle pan until smoking hot. Add the slices of bread and chargrill for 1–2 minutes on each side until nicely marked. Arrange on warmed plates and top with little gem lettuce leaves, the coriander sprigs and the wasabi salmon burgers. Spoon over the red onion salsa and garnish with lime wedges to serve.

Chef's top tip –
These burgers are flavoured with wasabi, which is a Japanese horseradish available in tubes from the Oriental section. It gives a fantastic kick to the fish, however you could use Dijon mustard instead.

CHEF RECIPE — **FEARGAL QUINN,**
FOUNDER & NON EXECUTIVE
PRESIDENT OF SUPERQUINN

potted
FLAVOUR

Feargal Quinn's garlic mussels with bay leaves

"The amounts in this recipe can easily be altered depending on how many guests you have. I tend to buy at least 1lb per person (a friend of mine would eat more than 100!)"

Serves 4

25 g (1 oz) butter

6 garlic cloves, finely chopped (trust me!)

6 shallots, finely chopped

½ bottle white wine

1 tbsp Dijon mustard

1.75 kg (4 lb) mussels, cleaned (see tip below)

6 bay leaves

crusty bread, to serve

Wine match
Australian Chardonnay
The light Chardonnay extends the creaminess of this dish.

To download the shopping list:
www.superquinn.ie/content/GarlicMussels
WithBayLeaves/955

1   Melt the butter a large pot with a lid. Add the garlic and shallots and gently simmer for a few minutes until softened but not coloured, stirring occasionally.

2   Pour in the white wine and add the mustard. Bring to a simmer and gently tip in the mussels and tuck in the bay leaves, then cover with a lid and cook for a minute or two until all the mussels have opened. Discard any that do not.

3   Remove from heat and let all the flavours mingle, then ladle into bowls with plenty of the liquor and serve with a separate bowl of crusty bread for mopping up.

chef's top tip —
Wash the mussels in plenty of cold water and scrub the shells with a stiff brush. Use a knife to scrape off any barnacles that are sticking to them. Discard any that do not close when lightly tapped on the work surface. Pull out the tough, fibrous beards protruding from the tightly closed shells.

crispWRAPPER

The batter for the plaice is wonderfully crisp and is based on a Japanese-style tempura batter. Always choose fresh fish that has no odour and looks translucent with nice firm flakes.

Crispy plaice with salsa verde mayonnaise

Serves 4

2 litres (3 ½ pints) vegetable oil

4 x 250 g (9 oz) plaice fillets, skinned

100 g (4 oz) plain flour

100 g (4 oz) cornflour

350 ml (12 fl oz) iced sparkling water

For the salsa verde mayonnaise:

120 ml (4 fl oz) mayonnaise (home-made or shop-bought)

1 garlic clove, crushed

1 shallot, finely chopped

2 tbsp capers, rinsed

2 tbsp chopped fresh flat-leaf parsley

1 tsp Dijon mustard

½ lemon, pips removed, plus extra wedges to garnish

Maldon sea salt and freshly ground black pepper

To download the shopping list: www.superquinn.ie/content/CrispyPlaiceWith SalsaVerdeMayonnaise/956

1 To make the salsa verde mayonnaise, place the mayonnaise in a bowl and stir in the garlic, shallot, capers, parsley and mustard. Stir in enough lemon juice to taste and season generously. Transfer to a serving bowl and cover with cling film, then chill until ready to serve.

2 Pour all the vegetable oil into a deep-sided pan, making sure it is only half full, or use a deep fat fryer. Heat to 190°C (375°F) or until a small piece of white bread dropped into the oil browns and rises to the surface in 1 minute. To make the tempura batter, mix together the flour and cornflour in a bowl with a pinch of salt and then whisk in the iced sparkling water. Do not worry about lumps, as these will improve the texture of the batter, which needs to be used straight away.

3 Cut the skinned plaice fillets into 4 cm (1 ½ in) strips on the diagonal and then quickly dip in the batter. Lower into the heated oil and cook for 3–4 minutes or until the fish is cooked through and the batter is crisp and golden. Drain briefly on kitchen so the batter doesn't loose any of its crispness and season lightly with salt. Transfer to warmed plates and add a spoonful of the salsa verde mayonnaise, the remainder can be served separately. Garnish with lemon wedges to serve.

Wine match
New Zealand Chardonnay
The light lemony tone of the New Zealand Chardonnay will compliment the delicate flavour of the plaice without overpowering it.

for
food
LOVERS

Pacific oysters are larger than our native oysters, with long oval shells and are very good indeed. They are spawned in warm waters and transferred to beds around Ireland, so are therefore available all year round, but are at their best from October to March when they are at their most succulent.

Champagne oysters

Serves 4

24 rock oysters (farmed, Pacific)

225 ml (8 fl oz) Champagne

1 shallot, finely chopped

225 ml (8 fl oz) double cream

about 450 g (1 lb) coarse sea salt

2 tsp snipped fresh chives

freshly ground white pepper

To download the shopping list:
www.superquinn.ie/content/Champagne
Oysters/957

① Scrub the oyster shells well then place one, wrapped in a clean tea towel, on a firm surface with the flattest shell uppermost and the hinge pointing towards you. Gripping the oyster firmly, insert an oyster knife into the gap in the hinge and twist to snap the shells apart.

② Slide the blade of the knife along the inside of the upper shell to sever the muscle that keeps the shells together. Lift the lid off the top shell, being careful not to spill any of the juices. Carefully clean away any bits of broken shell and finally run the knife under the oyster to loosen it from the shell. Repeat until all the oysters are opened.

③ Place the Champagne and shallot in a pan over a medium heat and bring to the boil. Reduce the heat to medium-low and simmer for 4-5 minutes or until reduced by half. Stir in the cream and season with white pepper. Simmer again for 3-4 minutes or until reduced by half and the sauce is thick and creamy, stirring occasionally.

④ Preheat the grill to high. Divide the coarse sea salt among four small heatproof dishes and arrange the oysters on the sea salt. Spoon the cream mixture evenly among the oysters. Cook under the grill for 1-2 minutes or until bubbling and golden. Set aside for 2 minutes to cool slightly, then scatter over the chives to serve.

chef's top tip –

If you pop your oysters into the microwave for 2 seconds, they start to open up a little and then are much easier to get a knife into to open up.

Wine match
Champagne
There really is only one perfect match for the Champagne in this dish and that is Champagne!

CHEF RECIPE — ROSS LEWIS,
CHAPTER ONE,
DUBLIN

stream LINES

Poached organic salmon salad

"The essential point of this dish is not to exceed the cooking times of the salmon so that the flesh is beautifully succulent. It really is very simple to make and careful presentation really adds effect."

Serves 4

100 g (4 oz) organic salmon fillets, skinned and boned

300 g (11 oz) new potatoes, scrubbed clean

about 150 ml (¼ pint) olive oil

1 tbsp chopped fresh mixed basil and chives

100 g (4 oz) French green beans, bottom ends trimmed

100 g (4 oz) tender asparagus tips

2 sun-dried tomatoes in oil, drained and chopped

1 tsp capers, rinsed

handful wild rocket leaves

½ lemon, pips removed

4 tsp herb mayonnaise (see Chef's top tip)

To download the shopping list:
www.superquinn.ie/content/Poached
OrganicSalmonSalad/958

For the court bouillon:

50 ml (2 fl oz) white wine vinegar

1 each carrot, celery stick and onion, chopped

1 fennel bulb, chopped

2 star anise

4 black peppercorns

1 bay leaf

1 sprig each fresh thyme, dill, tarragon and basil

Maldon sea salt and freshly ground white pepper

Wine match
Chablis Premier Cru
The elegance of this dish requires an elegant wine like the Chablis Premier Cru.

1　To make the court bouillon, place all the ingredients in a pan with 1.5 litres (2 ½ pints) of water. Bring to the boil, then add the salmon and remove from the heat. Set aside for 25 minutes until the salmon is just cooked through but still pink and succulent in the middle.

2　Cook the potatoes in a pan of boiling salted water until tender. Drain and peel while still warm, then roughly crush with a fork and gently work in about six tablespoons of the olive oil. Season to taste and fold in the herbs.

3　Blanch the French beans and asparagus tips in separate pans of salted water, then quickly refresh in cold water and drain. Gently split each French bean in half.

4　Spoon the crushed potatoes into a 10 cm (4 in) cutter set on plates and gently press down. Arrange the poached salmon on top. Scatter the French beans and asparagus tips around the plate and then sprinkle over the sun-dried tomatoes, capers and rocket. Mix the rest of the olive oil with a squeeze of lemon juice and season to taste, then use to dress the vegetables. Drizzle over the herb mayonnaise to serve.

Chef's top tip —

To make your own herb mayonnaise, blanch 15 g (½ oz) each of watercress, chervil, flat-leaf parsley and tarragon leaves for 1 minute, then refresh and squeeze dry. Place in a mini blender with an egg yolk, 1 tsp each of Dijon mustard and white wine vinegar and 150 ml (¼ pint) of olive oil. Blitz until you have a thick mayonnaise and pass through a sieve if you want a really smooth finish.

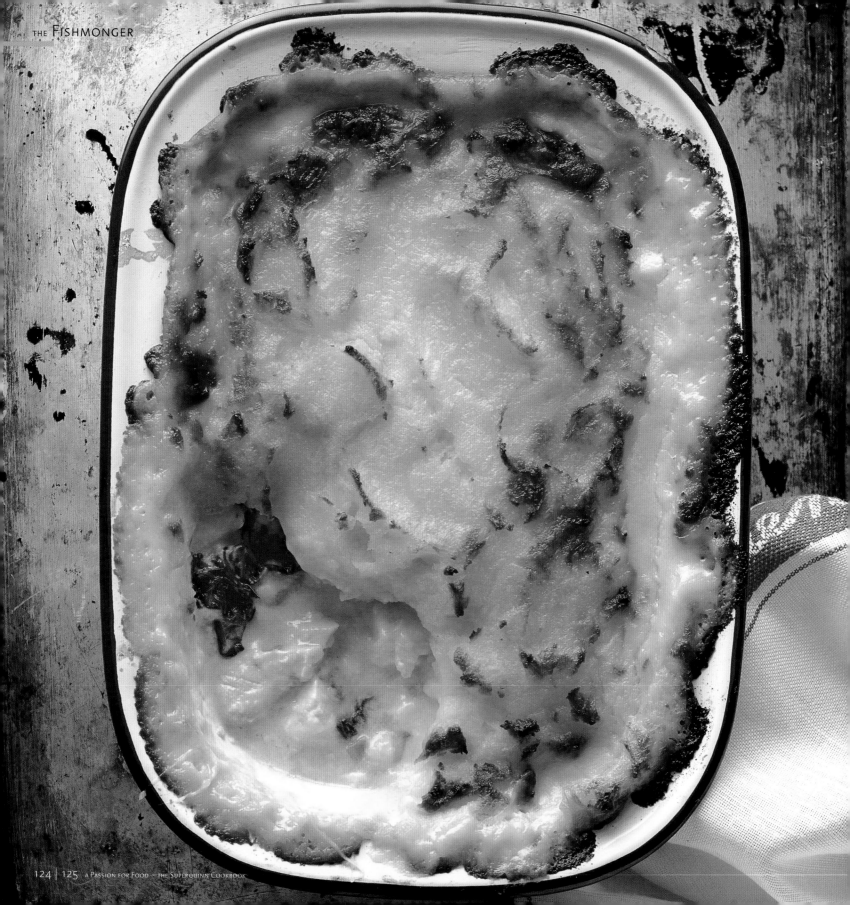

STAFF RECIPE — BRUCE LANGLANDS,
SUPERQUINN HEAD OFFICE

PIE in the sky

Bruce's fish pie

"Don't be afraid to experiment with the combination of fish, but don't be tempted to use more than half the quantity of smoked fish or its flavour will overpower."

BRUCE is head of New Product Development at Superquinn. This recipe has been perfected by him over a number of years and always has his guests begging for more!

Wine match
Sancerre
The gentle, slightly buttery tone of the Sancerre works very well with the creaminess of this fish pie.

Serves 4 – 6

550 g (1 ¼ lb) potatoes, cut into chunks

75 g (3 oz) butter

450 ml (¾ pint) milk

3 eggs

2 large shallots

2 celery sticks

2 bay leaves

few black peppercorns

750 g (1 ¾ lb) mixture un-dyed smoked haddock, fresh salmon and cod fillets

2 tbsp plain flour

200 g packet baby spinach leaves

Maldon sea salt and freshly ground white pepper

To download the shopping list:
www.superquinn.ie/content/FishPie/959

1 Cook the potatoes in a pan of salted water for 15–20 minutes until tender. Drain and mash until smooth with half of the butter and enough of the milk to give a creamy but firm consistency. Place the eggs in a pan with water and simmer for 10–12 minutes until hard-boiled, then shell and roughly chop.

2 Roughly chop one of the shallots and celery sticks and place in a wide pan with the milk, bay leaves, and peppercorns. Lower in the fish fillets, then bring to the boil and simmer for 3 minutes or until the fish is just tender. Transfer to a plate, then roughly flake, discarding the skin and bones. Strain the milk – you'll need 350 ml (12 fl oz) for the sauce.

3 Heat a knob of butter in a pan. Add fistfuls of the spinach, adding another as one wilts down. Cook for 1 minute, then tip into a colander to drain. Wipe out the pan and add the rest of the butter. Finely chop the remaining shallot and celery and add, stirring to coat. Sauté for 3–4 minutes then add the flour and stir over a low heat for 1 minute. Gradually add the reserved milk, beating until smooth. Simmer for 2–3 minutes until nicely thickened. Season to taste.

4 Preheat the oven to 180C (350°F), Gas mark 4. Layer up the flaked fish and hard-boiled eggs in an ovenproof dish with small mounds of the spinach and spoonfuls of the sauce. Spread the mashed potatoes on top and bake for 25–30 minutes until bubbling and golden. Serve the fish pie straight to the table.

Chef's top tip –
For the best results choose fish fillets from the centre cut as they will cook more evenly.

Fish & TIPS

This makes a nice change from your average bowl of pasta and is perfect when you want something special but don't have a lot of time on your hands.

Spaghetti with seafood

Serves 4

1.5 kg (3 lb) mussels

2 tbsp dry white wine

350 g (12 oz) spaghetti

4 tbsp extra virgin olive oil

2 garlic cloves, very finely chopped

1 red chilli, seeded and finely chopped

2 small squid, cleaned and cut into thin rings

350 g (12 oz) raw prawns, peeled and veins removed

200 g (7 oz) cherry tomatoes, halved

2 tbsp chopped fresh flat-leaf parsley

salt and freshly ground black pepper

To download the shopping list:
www.superquinn.ie/content/
SpaghettiWithSeafood/960

1   Clean the mussels (see Chef's top tip, page 119) and place in a pan with a lid and pour over the wine. Cover tightly and cook over a high heat for a few minutes, shaking the pan occasionally until all the mussels have opened – discard any that do not. Strain through a sieve, reserving 150 ml (¼ pint) of the cooking liquor, leaving behind any grit. Reserve a few mussels for garnish and remove the remainder from their shells.

2   Meanwhile, twirl the spaghetti into a pan of boiling salted water; stir once and then cook for 8–10 minutes until 'al dente' or according to instructions on the packet.

3   Heat the oil in a heavy-based frying pan and add the garlic and chilli, then sauté for about 30 seconds until lightly golden. Add the squid and cook gently for a few minutes, then tip in the prawns and sauté for another minute or so until just sealed. Add the reserved cooking liquid and reduce slightly, then tip in the mussels, tomato halves and parsley. Season to taste and allow to just warm through.

4   Drain the pasta and then return to the pan, then pour in the seafood sauce and fold together until well combined. Divide among warmed wide-rimmed bowls and serve at once.

Wine match
Australian Pinot Grigio
The crispness of a Pinot Grigio counters the richness of the seafood.

sauce PAN

> This dish would also be delicious with salmon. The smoky sweetness really intensifies as the sauce is reduced, while the chilli gives a wonderful bite.

Monkfish teriyaki style with noodle salad

Serves 4

300 g (10 oz) Chinese egg noodles

1 tbsp toasted sesame oil

3 tbsp chopped fresh coriander, plus extra to garnish

grated rind and juice of lime

3 tbsp sunflower oil, plus extra for brushing

1 large garlic clove, grated

1 cm (½ in) piece fresh root ginger, peeled and grated

1 red chilli, seeded and finely chopped

5 tbsp dark soy sauce

2 tbsp maple syrup

2 x 200 g (7 oz) monkfish fillets, trimmed and each cut into 3 medallions

To download the shopping list:
www.superquinn.ie/content/MonkfishTeriyaki
StyleWithNoodleSalad/961

Wine match
New Zealand Pinot Noir
Monkfish is a meatier fish and the teriyaki style of this dish allows it to be matched with a light red like a New Zealand Pinot Noir.

1 Place the noodles in a pan of boiling salted water and cook for 3 minutes until just tender. Drain and refresh quickly under cold running water. Return to the pan and stir in the sesame oil, coriander and add one teaspoon of the lime juice. Set aside until needed.

2 Heat half the sunflower oil a heavy-based frying pan. Add the garlic, ginger and chilli and sauté for 1 minute, then add the lime rind and remaining juice, the soy sauce and maple syrup and cook for another minute until slightly reduced and sticky.

3 Meanwhile, place in a heavy-based frying pan over a medium-low heat and add the rest of the sunflower oil. Add the monkfish medallions and cook for 2–3 minutes on each side until just cooked through and tender, then spoon over and swirl around the teriyaki sauce to coat the monkfish completely.

4 Arrange the noodles in the centre of warmed plates and arrange three monkfish medallions on each plate, spooning around any remaining teriyaki sauce. Garnish with coriander and serve at once.

Chef's top tip —

Ask at the fishmonger counter to remove all the membrane that encases the fillets of monkfish otherwise it will shrink during cooking, causing the fish to twist unattractively.

shell OUT

Dublin Bay prawns actually look a lot like small slender lobsters, with rather more delicate colouring and lighter claws in relation to the body. They may seem like an expensive luxury but are well worth every cent. At their best from late spring to late autumn, they need very little effort to make a stunning meal.

Sizzling Dublin Bay prawns with chilli and garlic

Serves 4

20 large Dublin Bay prawns

4 tbsp olive oil

knob of butter

1 red chilli, halved, seeded and cut into rings

1 garlic clove, thinly sliced

½ lemon, pips removed

1 tbsp chopped fresh flat-leaf parsley

Maldon sea salt and freshly ground black pepper

crusty bread, to serve

To download the shopping list:
www.superquinn.ie/content/SizzlingDublinBay
PrawnsWithChilliAndGarlic/962

1 To prepare the prawns, firmly twist the head away from the body and discard, or use for stock. Turn each prawn over and crack open the hard shell along the belly, then carefully peel it away from the flesh, twisting off the tail.

2 To remove the intestinal tract, which looks like a thin black vein running down the back of the prawn flesh, run the tip of a small knife down the back of each prawn and then lift up and pull out the vein. If you are lucky sometimes the vein comes away with the prawn tail or can be easily pulled out without having to cut the prawn at all.

3 Heat the olive oil in a large frying pan with the knob of butter. Once the butter has stopped sizzling, add the chilli and garlic and sauté for about 30 seconds until the garlic is lightly golden. Tip in the prepared prawns and sauté for another few minutes until tender. The prawns will change in colour and begin to curl into a prawn shape. Be careful not to over cook. Add a good squeeze of lemon juice and sprinkle over the parsley, tossing to coat. Season to taste and divide among warmed dishes with all of their delicious juices. Serve at once with plenty of crusty bread.

Wine match
New Zealand Sauvignon Blanc
The fruity, citrus tones of the New Zealand Sauvignon Blanc really live up to the power of the chilli and the garlic in this dish.

HOME COOK RECIPE — DONAL SKEHAN,
www.thegoodmoodfoodblog.com

scaleHEIGHTS

Mackerel with chilli, garlic and bulgar wheat salad

Serves 4

4 large mackerel fillets, scaled

olive oil, for cooking

1 lemon, halved (pips removed), plus extra wedges to garnish

2 red chillies, seeded and finely chopped

4 garlic cloves, finely chopped

For the bulgar wheat salad:

200 g (7 oz) bulgar wheat

1 tsp vegetable bouillon powder

15 g packet fresh flat-leaf parsley, leaves stripped and roughly chopped

15 g (½ oz) rocket, roughly chopped

75 g (3 oz) cherry tomatoes, quartered

400 g can chickpeas, drained and roughly chopped

1 tbsp balsamic vinegar

3 tbsp extra virgin olive oil

Maldon sea salt and freshly ground black pepper

To download the shopping list:
www.superquinn.ie/content/Mackerel
WithChilli GarlicAndBulgarWheatSalad/963

"For me, mackerel dishes always have to be simple with really fresh flavours, and I just love this quick recipe, which has a great kick of heat thanks to the chilli. People get a bit worried when it comes to cooking fish, but go to the fish counter and ask them to do all the hard work and you will be left with really lovely fillets of fish, which are no more complicated to cook than a chicken breast!"

1. To make the salad, place the bulgar wheat in a large bowl and cover with boiling water. Stir through the vegetable bouillon powder, cover with cling film and allow to stand until all the water is soaked up and the bulgar wheat is soft and tender. Stir in the parsley, rocket, cherry tomatoes and chickpeas. Season and dress with the balsamic and olive oil. Cover with cling film and set aside until needed.

2. Place the mackerel fillets on a large plate and drizzle with olive oil and a good squeeze of lemon juice. Don't use all the lemon juice here, as it's nice to give the fish an extra squeeze of lemon while it cooks. Sprinkle over the chillies and garlic and gently rub into the fish on both sides, turning to coat.

3. Heat a non-stick griddle pan until smoking hot. Season the fillets and cook over a high heat, for 2–3 minutes either side until they are cooked through. Halfway through the cooking time, give them another splash of lemon juice. Arrange on plates with the bulgar wheat salad and add lemon wedges to garnish.

Wine match
Southern French Rosé
White wine with fish is a frequent rule but the bold flavours in this dish are complimented perfectly with a rosé.

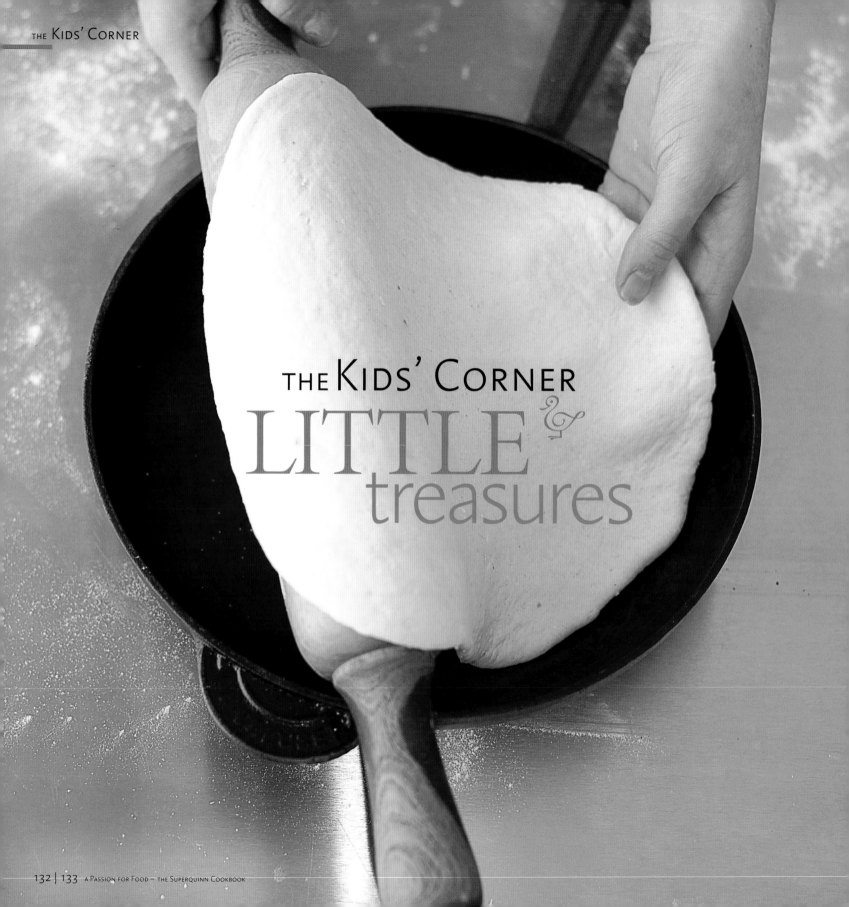

THE KIDS' CORNER
LITTLE &
treasures

THE KIDS' CORNER

We know that when kids eat a balanced, healthy diet they behave better, can concentrate more at school and have more energy for sport and play. And what better way to get them to eat well than getting them involved in the importance of what they eat. No-one understands this better than Superquinn's charity partner Barretstown, a unique therapeutic recreation camp for children with cancer and other serious illnesses and their families. Inside you will find some of their most popular recipes.

Everyone knows that kids love to be involved, young ones can roll their sleeves up at the sink, apron on, and wash the salad leaves and vegetables, while older ones can help peel and stir a sauce. The main thing is to involve them in the process and explain what you're doing while you're cooking. That way they'll be more curious to taste the finished product, and you could end up with a budding chef on your hands!

Kids also love miniature things made to be eaten with little fingers. So mini sandwiches and grilled fruit kebabs are always sure to please.

one BY one

These fruit kebabs are just wonderful cooked on the gentle embers of a barbecue as a dessert but work equally well under the grill or on a griddle pan if you don't get the weather!

Grilled fruit kebabs

Makes 16 small kebabs

2 tbsp sunflower oil

2 tbsp light muscovado sugar

4 tbsp fresh lime juice

good pinch of ground cinnamon

1 tbsp chopped fresh mint

2 apples, cored and cut into 8 pieces

2 large bananas, peeled and each cut into 8 pieces

2 plums, stoned and cut into 8 pieces

4 kiwi fruit, peeled and each cut into 4 pieces

16 large chunks of fresh pineapple

16 strawberries, hulled

To download the shopping list:
www.superquinn.ie/contentGrilledFruitKebabs/964

1 Place the sunflower oil, sugar, lime juice, cinnamon and mint in a small bowl and stir until the sugar has dissolved.

2 Thread the fruit onto 16 small metal skewers or soaked wooden ones in an attractive fashion, then brush all over with the sugar glaze.

3 Heat a griddle pan, the barbecue or a grill. Put the kebabs on to cook and cook for 6–8 minutes, turning and basting frequently until the fruit starts to caramelise. Arrange on plates or a large platter to serve.

Chef's top tip –

For a really special treat, serve with a chocolate fondue. Melt your favourite chocolate with a couple of tablespoons of cream in a small pan or in the microwave, stirring until smooth.

BITE sized

These small sandwiches, in a chequerboard design are just perfect for little fingers to pick up. If you really want to push the boat out decorate with mini flags on cocktail sticks.

Chequerboard sandwiches

Serves 8–10

16 thin slices white bread

16 thin slices brown bread

75 g (3 oz) butter, at room temperature

20 slices ham

To download the shopping list:
www.superquinn.ie/content/Chequerboard
Sandwiches/965

Chef's top tip –

Of course you can experiment with the fillings of these sandwiches, try thinly sliced cucumber, Cheddar, tomato or egg mayonnaise which would all work well, depending on what your children enjoy eating.

1 Spread all but two of the slices of bread thinly with butter (reserve one white and one brown) and then cover one-third with a layer of ham. Top with another slice of bread that is the same colour and put slices of ham on top. Cover with the rest of the buttered bread (again, using the same colour) and then trim off all the crusts so that you end up with even-sized squares.

2 Cut each triple sandwich square into four and then arrange on large flat plate or coloured napkin in layers of six, alternating between white and brown sandwiches to represent a chequerboard (you will have a couple of sandwiches leftover at the end – cook's treat!).

3 Stamp out 1 cm (½ in) rounds from the reserved slices of bread and arrange on the sandwich chequerboard so that they represent chips. Wrap in cling film and store in the fridge for up to 6 hours and allow to come back to room temperature before serving.

made to DISAPPEAR

All children seem to just love meatballs and these ones taste particularly delicious. Serve them with spaghetti as suggested here or use to fill pitta breads with shredded lettuce, diced tomatoes and a squeeze of mayonnaise.

Marvellous meatballs with spaghetti

Serves 4

225 g (8 oz) lean minced beef

225 g (8 oz) minced pork

8 Jacob's cream crackers, crushed into fine crumbs

1 tbsp chopped fresh flat-leaf parsley

1 egg

2 tbsp olive oil, plus extra for drizzling

1 onion, finely chopped

1 celery stick, finely chopped

1 large garlic clove, crushed

500 ml bottle passata (Italian sieved tomatoes)

2 tbsp tomato purée

350 g (12 oz) spaghetti

25 g (1 oz) freshly grated Parmesan

salt and freshly ground black pepper

To download the shopping list:
www.superquinn.ie/content/Marvellous MeatballsWithSpaghetti/966

1 Place the minced beef and pork in a bowl with the cream crackers, parsley and egg. Season to taste and using your hands give everything a good mix. Using slightly wetted hands, make about 20 even-sized balls. Arrange on a flat baking sheet, drizzle over a little olive oil to lightly coat and chill for an hour to firm up if time allows.

2 Heat half the olive oil in a large pan and sauté the onion and celery for about 5 minutes until lightly golden. Stir in the garlic and cook for another minute, stirring. Add the passata and tomato purée and simmer for a few minutes until nicely combined. Season to taste.

3 Heat the rest of the olive oil in a deep-sided frying pan and sauté the meatballs for 8–10 minutes until almost cooked through and nicely browned. Pour in the sauce and simmer gently for another 10 minutes or so until the meatballs are completely tender and the sauce has reduced and thickened.

4 Meanwhile, plunge the spaghetti into a large pan of boiling salted water and simmer for 8–10 minutes until tender but still with a little bite, as the Italians say 'al dente'. Drain well and return to the pan and then add a few ladlefuls of the tomato sauce to coat. Divide among warmed bowls and spoon the meatballs with the rest of the tomato sauce on top. Scatter over the Parmesan to serve.

HEY
pesto

This pesto will keep well in the fridge for up to one week – just keep it topped up with a little extra olive oil to ensure that it stays lovely and fresh.

Roly-poly ravioli with fresh pesto sauce

Serves 4

25 g (1 oz) pine nuts

2 x 300 g packets roasted tomato, mozzarella & basil ravioli

1 garlic clove, peeled

25 g (1 oz) fresh basil leaves

25 g (1 oz) freshly grated Parmesan

6 tbsp olive oil, plus a little extra if necessary

Maldon sea salt and freshly ground black pepper

To download the shopping list:
www.superquinn.ie/content/RolyPoly
RavioliWithFreshPestoSauce/967

1 Preheat the oven to 180°C (350°F), Gas mark 4. Place the pine nuts in a baking tin and roast for 6–8 minutes or until nicely toasted. Remove from the oven and leave to cool.

2 Bring a large pan of salted water to the boil. Add the tomato and mozzarella ravioli, give it a good stir and simmer for 3–4 minutes according to packet instructions.

3 Place the cooled pine nuts in a food processor with the garlic, basil and Parmesan. Season to taste and pour in the olive oil. Blitz to a thick purée adding a little more olive oil if necessary.

4 Drain the pasta and return to the pan and then stir in the pesto until evenly combined. Divide among warmed plates and serve at once.

Chef's top tip –

To make your own sun-dried tomato pesto, simply replace half the quantity of basil with semi sun-dried or sun blush tomatoes.

NAME THAT tuna

This is a great recipe for children, especially when you have nothing much in the house. To make your own sweet chilli sauce, mix four tablespoons of tomato ketchup with a tablespoon of clear honey, a quarter teaspoon of chilli powder and the juice of half a lime.

Golden tuna fish triangles

Serves 4

450 g (1 lb) potatoes, cut into cubes

200 g can tuna in brine, drained

4 spring onions, finely chopped

2 tbsp chopped fresh flat-leaf parsley

4 tbsp soured cream

finely grated rind of 1 lime

2 tbsp sunflower oil

1 tbsp plain flour

salt and freshly ground black pepper

**sweet chilli sauce, to serve
(see introduction)**

To download the shopping list:
www.superquinn.ie/content/GoldenTuna
FishTriangles/968

1 Cook the potatoes in a pan of boiling salted water for 10–12 minutes until tender. Drain and mash well, then fold in the tuna, spring onions, parsley, soured cream and lime rind. Season to taste. Divide into eight portions and shape into triangles.

2 Heat the oil in a non-stick frying pan. Dust the fish triangles with flour and then add to the pan. Cook for 2–3 minutes on each side until golden and drain on kitchen paper. Serve on plates with a spoonful of sweet chilli sauce.

choc -a- BLOCK

This is a great recipe to make with the children; it's just hard to stop them eating it before it goes into a tin! The finished brownies can also be cut into bite-sized pieces if you prefer and would make a lovely present wrapped in tissue paper in a nice box.

Melted chocolate rocky road brownies

Makes about 12

4 x 58 g Mars bars

4 tbsp pouring golden syrup

100 g (4 oz) butter

50 g (2 oz) rice crispies

40 g Crunchie bar, finely chopped

50 g (2 oz) mini marshmallows

100g bar plain or milk chocolate, broken into squares

To download the shopping list:
www.superquinn.ie/content/Melted
ChocolateRockyRoadBrownies/969

Chef's top tip –

If you don't want to use the Crunchie bar and mini marshmallows simply increase the rice crispies to 100 g (4 oz) and the recipe will still work fine.

1 Chop up the Mars bars into small pieces and place in a pan with the golden syrup and 75 g (3 oz) of the butter. Cook over a low heat for 3–4 minutes until melted, then beat until smooth. Leave to cool a little.

2 Fold the rice crispies into the Mars bar mixture with the Crunchie bar and mini marshmallows until well combined. Transfer to a 17.5 cm (7 in) shallow square tin that has been lined with parchment paper and spread out evenly with a spatula.

3 Melt the plain or milk chocolate with the rest of the butter in a heatproof bowl set over a pan of simmering water. Spread or drizzle in an even layer over the brownies and set aside for at least 1 hour until set. Cut into bars or squares and arrange on a plate to serve.

for cookie MONSTERS

These are perfect for handing out to children at the end of a barbecue or family gathering. If you don't want to serve them immediately they can be wrapped tightly in cling film and frozen until needed. It is also a nice idea to roll the sides of the ice cream cookie sandwiches in hundreds and thousands or crumbled up flake.

Ice cream cookie sandwiches

Makes about 10

225 g (8 oz) butter, at room temperature

375 g (13 oz) light muscovado sugar

2 eggs

2 tsp vanilla extract

350 g (12 oz) plain flour

1 tsp baking powder

1 tsp bread soda

½ tsp salt

120 g packet of Smarties

500 ml carton vanilla ice cream

To download the shopping list:
www.superquinn.ie/content/IceCream
CookieSandwiches/970

Chef's top tip –

If you don't want to go to the trouble of baking your own cookies use a packet of large chocolate chip cookies. Children will love them just as much!

1. Preheat the oven to 180°C (350°F), Gas mark 4. Using a hand-held mixer, cream the butter and sugar in a large bowl until soft and fluffy. Whisk the eggs lightly with the vanilla extract and then gradually beat into the butter mixture.

2. Sieve the flour, baking powder, bread soda and salt into a separate bowl, then beat into the butter and egg mixture.

3. Spoon tablespoons of the cookie mixture on to large non-stick baking sheets, allowing plenty of room for spreading. Dot with the Smarties and bake for 10–12 minutes until just golden brown around the edges but still pale golden in the centre – they will be still nice and chewy if you cook them like this.

4. Leave for a few minutes to settle, then using a metal fish slice or spatula, quickly transfer to a wire rack while they are still hot (otherwise they tend to stick). Leave to cool completely.

5. To serve, place a scoop of ice cream on the flat side of half of the cookies. Cover with the rest of the cookies then press each one down gently to make a sandwich. Serve at once.

CUSTOMER RECIPE — MARY MILLER,
SUPERQUINN PORTLAOISE

YELLOW belly

Banana & walnut bread

"This is a great recipe to use up over-ripe bananas. I just love the smell that fills the kitchen as it bakes and then it tastes even better! Why not double the quantities and make two, then you can pop one into the freezer or give it as a present."

MARY shops in Superquinn Portlaoise and has not shopped anywhere else since it opened in 2008. She is a keen baker but thinks that the quality of the cakes that Superquinn makes is excellent and often treats herself.

Makes 1 loaf

3 ripe bananas

100 ml (3 ½ fl oz) sunflower oil, plus extra for greasing

1 egg

100 g (4 oz) caster sugar

1 tsp vanilla extract

pinch of salt

1 tsp bread soda

100 g (4 oz) shelled walnuts, finely chopped

225 g (8 oz) plain flour

To download the shopping list:
www.superquinn.ie/content/Banana&
WalnutBread/973

1 Preheat the oven to 180°F (350°F), Gas mark 4. Peel and mash the bananas in a bowl and then mix in the sunflower oil until smooth. Beat in the egg, sugar and vanilla extract.

2 Add the salt to the banana mixture and then add the bread soda. Stir in the walnuts and finally using a large metal spoon, fold in the flour until well combined.

3 Pour the batter into an oiled 900 g (2 lb) non-stick loaf tin and bake for 1 hour or until well risen and golden brown. To test that the bread is cooked, push a thin skewer into the middle of the bread and if it comes out clean it is cooked.

4 Leave the banana & walnut bread to settle in the tin for 5 minutes, then transfer to a wire rack and leave to cool completely. Cut into slices and arrange on a plate to serve.

Chef's top tip —

Instead of using the vanilla extract make your own vanilla sugar. The next time you scrape out the vanilla seeds from a pod for a recipe give the pod a quick rinse and pat dry with kitchen paper. Pop into a bag of caster sugar and leave for a couple of weeks to allow the flavour to develop.

reach
for the PIE

If you think making pizzas takes loads of time and effort kneading and tossing, then try this recipe. The dough is actually very similar to soda bread but gets cooked directly on the hob and not in the oven.

Pan-fried pizza Italiana with chorizo

Serves 2–4

1 tbsp olive oil, plus extra for drizzling

1 garlic clove, crushed

400 g can plum tomatoes

1 tsp caster sugar

50 g (2 oz) sliced chorizo salami (from a packet or from the deli)

100 g ball mozzarella or Cheddar cheese, diced (or use a mixture)

For the dough:

225 g (8 oz) self-raising flour, plus extra for dusting

2 tbsp freshly grated Parmesan

2 tbsp olive oil

salt and freshly ground black pepper

fresh basil leaves, to garnish

To download the shopping list:
www.superquinn.ie/content/PanFried
PizzaItalianaWithChorizo/972

Chef's top tip –

Of course you can invent your own flavour combination for the topping. Choose from olives, ham, cooked bacon, pepperoni, pineapple or mushrooms.

1 To make the tomato sauce, heat the olive oil in a pan and add the garlic and tomatoes. Break up with a wooden spoon or a potato masher. Add the sugar and season to taste. Then cook for 8–10 minutes, stirring regularly until most of the juice has evaporated and the sauce has nicely thickened.

2 To make the dough, sift the flour into a bowl with a pinch of salt, then stir in the Parmesan. Make a well in the centre and stir in 150 ml (¼ pint) of warm water and one tablespoon of oil to make a soft dough. Roll out to a 25 cm (10 in) round on a lightly floured surface.

3 Preheat the grill and heat the remaining olive oil in an ovenproof frying pan. Add the dough and cook for 5–6 minutes until the underside is golden brown. While the dough is cooking, spoon over the tomato sauce and scatter over the chorizo and cheese. Drizzle over a little olive oil and place under a medium grill for 3–4 minutes until the top is golden and the base is cooked through. Garnish with the basil leaves and cut into wedges, then arrange on warmed plates to serve.

CHEF RECIPE — DECLAN FURLONG, BARRETSTOWN

SERIOUSLY yummy

Barretstown muesli cookies

"These energy rich cookies are a perfect treat for a breakfast on the go. With their low G.I., oatmeal content and punchy protein from the nuts, they are perfect to keep children alert and ready to face the day ahead. For an extra luxury add a handful of chocolate chips."

Makes about 20

100 g (4 oz) butter, plus extra for greasing

75 g (3 oz) light muscovado sugar

75 g (3 oz) crunchy peanut butter

1 egg

50 g (2 oz) plain flour

½ tsp baking powder

½ tsp ground cinnamon

pinch of salt

225 g (8 oz) muesli

50 g (2 oz) raisins

50 g (2 oz) shelled walnuts, chopped

To download the shopping list:
www.superquinn.ie/content/Barretstown
MuesliCookies/971

1 Preheat the oven to 180°C (350°F), Gas mark 4. Place the butter and sugar in a bowl and using a hand-held mixer, cream together until light and fluffy. Beat in the peanut butter and then beat in the egg.

2 Sift the flour, baking powder, cinnamon and salt into a separate bowl and then beat into the peanut butter mixture. Fold in the muesli, raisins and walnuts until well combined.

3 Drop rounded tablespoons of the cookie mixture on to greased baking sheets about 2.5 cm (1 in) apart to allow for spreading. Press gently with the back of a spoon to spread each mound into a circle. Bake for 15 minutes until just cooked through and lightly golden. Using a metal fish slice or spatula, transfer to a wire rack and leave to cool. Arrange on a plate to serve.

BLOWING raspberries

Barretstown raspberry muffins

"All children love muffins and enjoy getting stuck in when it comes to baking. You could also add dried cranberries or raisins instead of the raspberries."

Makes 12

50 g (2 oz) butter

100 g (4 oz) raspberries

25 g (1 oz) icing sugar, plus extra for dusting

275 g (10 oz) plain flour

2 tsp baking powder

150 g (5 oz) light muscovado sugar

finely grated rind of 1 orange

1 egg

1 tsp vanilla extract

225 ml (8 fl oz) milk

To download the shopping list:
www.superquinn.ie/content/Barretstown
RaspberryMuffins/974

1 Preheat the oven to 180°C (350°F), Gas mark 4. Line a 12-hole muffin tin with paper cases. Melt the butter in a small pan or in the microwave, then leave to cool. Toss the raspberries in a bowl with the icing sugar to coat.

2 Sift the flour and baking powder in a bowl. Stir in the light muscovado sugar, orange rind and sugar dusted raspberries.

3 In a separate bowl, beat together the egg, vanilla extract, milk and cooled melted butter, then fold into the dry ingredients until just combined. Do not be tempted to over-mix.

4 Divide the muffin mixture among the paper cases and bake for 18–20 minutes until well risen and just firm. Transfer to a wire rack and leave to cool completely. Arrange on a plate and lightly dust with icing sugar to serve.

fíre MOUNTAIN

This can be made in one large dessert bowl but children find it so much more dramatic to be able to crack the caramel topping themselves with the back of their spoon.

Cracking volcano fruity whip

Serves 4 – 6

450 g (1 lb) mixed berries, such as strawberries, raspberries and blueberries

1 ripe mango, peeled and cut into bite-sized chunks

icing sugar, to taste (optional)

150 ml (¼ pint) cream

200 ml carton crème fraîche

175 g (6 oz) caster sugar

To download the shopping list:
www.superquinn.ie/content/Cracking
VolcanoFruityWhip/975

1 Cut any large strawberries into halves or quarters, depending on their size. Mix all the fruit together in a bowl and sieve over a dusting of icing sugar if you think the fruit needs it. Divide among sturdy dessert glasses.

2 Place the cream and crème fraîche in a bowl and whip until it holds soft peaks. Spoon over the fruit to cover completely and chill for at least 2 hours. This will help the caramel to set immediately on contact.

3 Place the sugar in a heavy-based pan with two tablespoons of water over a high heat, swirling the pan occasionally until the sugar has dissolved and then simmer without stirring until golden brown. Quickly pour it over the cream mixture and serve at once.

berry
GOOD

For any child, breakfast in a glass is the perfect way to start the day. If the fruit is nice and ripe there's no need to sweeten with sugar or honey, but that of course is a personal preference.

Brilliant blueberry smoothie

Serves 4

275 g (10 oz) frozen blueberries

600 ml (1 pint) natural yoghurt

1 tsp clear honey

To download the shopping list:
www.superquinn.ie/content/Brilliant
BlueberrySmoothie/976

1 Place the blueberries in a liquidizer with the yoghurt and honey and blend until smooth. Pour into tumbler glasses and serve immediately.

Ways to change –
Bionic Berry

Replace the blueberries with frozen mixed berries and place in the liquidizer with the yoghurt and honey and add the finely grated rind and juice of 1 orange.

Tropical Coconut

Place 275 ml (10 fl oz) frozen tropical fruit into the liquidizer with the juice of 1 lime, 400 g can of coconut milk and 350 ml (12 fl oz) of tropical fruit juice or freshly squeezed orange juice.

Kiwi Crush

Peel and slice 4 ripe kiwi fruit and place in a liquidizer with 4 tablespoons of elderflower cordial and 600 ml (1 pint) grapefruit juice. Add 175 g (6 oz) ice cubes and blend until smooth.

the SWEET LIFE ◆
BE tempted

THE SWEET LIFE ◆

When it comes to perfect puddings, keeping it simple is usually best. No one knows this better than Superquinn, famous for their delicious cakes and desserts.

You will never be caught out if you always keep a stock of the staples; fresh fruit, flour, eggs, butter and sugar. You can then whip up a simple crumble in minutes that will satisfy any sweet-tooth.

For something a little more decadent, who can resist the velvety embrace of a dark chocolate treat. There can be few things as sensually satisfying as sinking your teeth into a slice of rich chocolate torte, or perhaps a slice of the most decadent banoffee pie.

Then again the old favourites are such for good reason – they are the people-pleasers that we come back to time and again like traditional apple tart, creamy rice pudding and super-comforting bread and butter pudding.

Whatever your secret treat is, make sure you make enough to share.

famously RICH

This flourless chocolate torte keeps very well in the fridge for up to 3 days, and even improves with time as it becomes even more dense and rich. It is crucial to add the hazelnut meringue to the chocolate mixture in at least two batches. This ensures the chocolate mixture retains as much air as possible, giving the chocolate torte a wonderful velvety texture. This recipe is suitable for people on a gluten-free diet.

Chocolate torte with vanilla ice cream

Serves 6–8

175 g (6 oz) unsalted butter, plus extra for greasing

175 g (6 oz) hazelnuts

175 g (6 oz) plain chocolate, broken into pieces (at least 70% cocoa solids)

175 g (6 oz) golden caster sugar

6 eggs, separated

2 tbsp apricot jam

vanilla ice cream, to serve

Wine match
Rutherglen Muscat
The richness of this decadent desert is matched perfectly with the sweetness of the Muscat.

To download the shopping list:
www.superquinn.ie/content/Chocolate TorteWithVanillaIceCream/977

Chef's top tip –

If you want to make individual puddings; spoon the chocolate mixture into 120 ml (4 fl oz) greased ramekins and arrange on a baking sheet. Bake for 18-20 minutes until firm and set.

① Preheat the oven to 180°C (350°F), Gas mark 4. Lightly grease a 23 cm (9 in) non-stick spring-form cake tin that is no more than 7.5 cm (3 in) deep and line the base with parchment paper. Place the hazelnuts in a roasting tin and roast for 10 minutes until toasted but not burnt. Leave to cool, then tip them into a clean tea towel and rub off the skins. Transfer the nuts to a food processor and blend for 30 seconds until finely ground.

② Place the chocolate in a heatproof bowl set over a pan of simmering water and allow to melt, then remove the bowl from the pan and leave to cool. Place half of the sugar and the butter into a large bowl and using a hand-held mixer, beat together until pale and creamy. Beat in the egg yolks with the melted chocolate.

③ Whisk the egg whites in a separate bowl until you have achieved soft peaks, then whisk in the remaining sugar until stiff. Gently fold the ground hazelnuts into the meringue, then gently fold into the chocolate mixture in two batches. Spoon into the prepared tin and bake for 40–45 minutes or until a skewer pushed into the centre of the torte comes out clean.

④ Melt the apricot jam in a small pan or in the microwave and pass through a fine sieve into a bowl. Remove the torte from the oven and brush the top liberally with the sieved apricot jam, then leave to cool in the tin. Cut into slices and arrange on plates with scoops of the vanilla ice cream to serve.

tart with a HEART

Homemade apple tart – a winning combination of delicate sweet pastry filled with heavenly-scented apples, it simply can't be beaten.

The best apple tart

Serves 6–8

225 g (8 oz) plain flour, plus extra for dusting

2 tbsp icing sugar

100 g (4 oz) butter

2 large egg yolks

900 g (2 lb) Bramley cooking apples

100 g (4 oz) golden caster sugar

¼ tsp ground cinnamon

good pinch of ground cloves

1 tbsp milk

To download the shopping list:
www.superquinn.ie/content/TheBest
AppleTart/978

Wine match
Australian Riesling
The sweetness of the Australian Riesling is perfectly balanced with the sweetness of the apple tart.

Chef's top tip –

To ring in the changes, mix the apples with blackberries or try a mixture of rhubarb and strawberry.

① Sift the flour and icing sugar into a bowl. Using a round-bladed knife, work in the butter and then mix in the egg yolks with two to three tablespoons of ice-cold water until the dough just comes together. Wrap in cling film and chill for at least 30 minutes.

② Preheat the oven to 190°C (375°F), Gas mark 5. Lightly dust the work surface with flour. Divide the pastry into two portions, one slightly larger than the other, then roll out the larger piece until it's about 30 cm (12 in) in diameter. Use to line a 20 cm (8 in) pie dish or 23 cm (9 in) flat plate, gently pressing into the corners. Knock the sides with a round-bladed knife to give a decorative finish and place back in the fridge to chill while you prepare the apples.

③ Peel, core and slice the apples. Place in a large bowl with all but one tablespoon of the caster sugar and the cinnamon and cloves. Brush the edge of the pastry with a little milk. Mix together, then pile into the lined pie dish. Roll out the second piece of pastry into a circle slightly larger than the pie dish and use to cover the apples. Press the edges together to seal, then use a sharp knife to cut away any excess.

④ Crimp the edges of the tart with a round-bladed knife and using your fingers as a guide and then roll out the pastry scraps and cut into leaf shapes. Brush with milk and stick on top of the pie. Brush with milk and sprinkle with the rest of the sugar. Bake for 25–30 minutes, then reduce the oven to 180°C (350°F), Gas mark 4 and bake for 20–25 minutes until golden brown. Cut into slices and put on plates to serve.

CHEF RECIPE — NEVEN MAGUIRE,
MACNEAN HOUSE & RESTAURANT
BLACKLOIN, CO. CAVAN

ART of glass

Poached plums with amaretti and lemon mascarpone

"This stunning dessert will really impress your guests at a dinner party! However, it is actually extremely simple to prepare and can be done well in advance leaving you to enjoy your meal."

Serves 4

250 g tub mascarpone cheese

500 ml carton chilled custard

finely grated rind of 1 lemon

12 amaretti biscuits

For the poached plums:

150 ml (¼ pint) red wine

175 g (6 oz) golden caster sugar

1 cinnamon stick

1 star anise

1 vanilla pod, split in half and seeds scraped out

450 g (1 lb) ripe plums, halved, stoned and cut into slices

To download the shopping list:
www.superquinn.ie/content/PoachedPlums
WithAmarettiAndLemonMascarpone/979

① To poach the plums, place the wine in a pan with 150 ml (¼ pint) of water, the sugar, cinnamon, star anise and vanilla seeds. Slowly bring to the boil, then reduce the heat and simmer gently for 20–25 minutes until reduced by half and syrupy in texture.

② Add the plums to the wine mixture and simmer gently for another 2 minutes until softened but still holding their shape, stirring occasionally but being careful not to damage the plums. Remove from the heat and leave to cool completely.

③ Place the mascarpone in a bowl with the custard and lemon rind. Whip until the mixture is just holding its shape and soft peaks have formed.

④ Divide the cooled poached plums among Martini glasses and crumble the amaretti on top, reserving a little for decoration. Spoon over the lemon mascarpone to cover completely and then sprinkle with the rest of the reserved amaretti. Chill for 2 hours before serving set on plates.

Chef's top tip —
Use whatever fruits are in season for this dessert, such as pears, blackberries or even rhubarb would work well.

Wine match
Australian Riesling
The fruitiness of this desert calls for a sweet Riesling such as that from Australia.

CUSTOMER RECIPE — NELLIE O'DRISCOLL,
SUPERQUINN CARLOW

LORD of the pies

Banoffee pie

"This version of banoffee pie is the most delicious you'll ever taste. It really is incredibly easy to prepare and looks like you've gone to loads to trouble."

Serves 6

2 x 400 g cans condensed milk

400 g packet digestive biscuits

175 g (6 oz) butter

3 tbsp clear honey

2 large ripe bananas

250 ml carton cream

300 ml (½ pint) chilled custard (from a carton)

cocoa powder, for dusting

Wine match
Muscat
The stickiness and sweetness of this pie calls for an equally sweet wine like the Muscat.

To download the shopping list:
www.superquinn.ie/content/BanoffeePie/980

① Place the cans of condensed milk in a large pan with a lid and cover completely with water. Bring to a simmer and cook for 2 ½ hours, topping up with water as necessary. Remove from the heat and leave to cool completely. These will sit happily in the fridge unopened for up to 1 month.

② Place the digestive biscuits in a plastic bag and crush into fine crumbs using a rolling pin. Melt the butter in a pan with the honey and stir in the crushed biscuits. Press the mixture into the base and up the sides of a non-stick loose-bottomed cake tin that is 23 cm (9 in) wide and about 7.5 cm (3 in) deep. Chill for at least 15 minutes.

③ Peel the bananas and thinly slice. Open the cooled cans of condensed milk and spread the toffee over the set biscuit base and cover with the sliced bananas. Lightly whip the cream in a bowl until soft peaks form. Spoon the custard on top of the bananas and spread it out to make a seal with the edge of the biscuit base. Swirl the whipped cream on top attractively and chill for at least an hour.

④ To serve, lightly dust the banoffee pie with cocoa powder and then carefully remove from the cake tin. Place on a cake stand, then cut into slices and arrange on plates to serve.

NELLIE lives in Cork but always shops in Superquinn Carlow when she stays with her son. A mother of four boys Nellie has always loved cooking and experimenting in the kitchen.

pear SHAPES

This dessert is perfect for a cold winter's day and you could use honey instead of the golden syrup. It would also be delicious served with some custard.

Flambé of pears with pecans and golden syrup

Serves 4

4 large ripe pears

juice of ½ lemon

50 g (2 oz) butter

25 g (1 oz) pecan nuts, roughly chopped

4 tbsp golden syrup

icing sugar, to dust

crème fraîche, to serve

Wine match
Muscat
The sweetness of the Muscat accentuates the nutty, toffee flavours of this desert.

To download the shopping list:
www.superquinn.ie/content/FlambeOfPears
WithPecansAndGoldenSyrup/981

1 Peel the pears and then cut each one into quarters, discarding the cores. Toss in the lemon juice to prevent them from going brown.

2 Heat a heavy-based frying pan over a medium heat. Add the butter and when it starts to foam, add the pear quarters. Cook for 1–2 minutes on each side until tender and lightly golden.

3 Scatter over the pecan nuts and then drizzle in the golden syrup. Cook for another minute or two until a nice toffee-like sauce has formed.

4 Divide the pears among warmed plates and spoon over the pecan nut sauce. Decorate with a dusting of icing sugar and then add a dollop of crème fraîche to each one to serve.

FOOL'S gold

You could buy some nice crisp ginger biscuits but to make your own is so much nicer. This recipe makes about 12 biscuits but you could easily double the quantity and store the remainder in an airtight tin. If they get the chance, they keep for up to 2 weeks.

Mango fool with stem ginger biscuits

Serves 4

2 ripe mangoes

1 lime

150 ml (¼ pint) cream

6 tbsp Greek style yoghurt

For the stem ginger biscuits:

50 g (2 oz) butter

1 tbsp golden syrup

1 tbsp golden caster sugar

75 g (3 oz) self-raising flour

½ tsp ground ginger

25 g (1 oz) crystallized stem ginger, finely chopped

Wine match
Australian Sparkling Wine
Match the frothy sweetness of this desert with a sweet sparkling wine from the New World.

To download the shopping list:
www.superquinn.ie/content/MangoFool
WithStemGingerBiscuits/982

① Peel the mangoes and then cut the flesh into a food processor, discarding the stones. Cut the lime in half and squeeze in the juice, then blend to a smooth purée.

② Place the cream in a bowl and whip until soft peaks form, then fold in the Greek yoghurt. Finally fold in the mango puree until just combined. Spoon the mixture into dessert glasses and chill for about 2 hours.

③ Meanwhile make the biscuits. Preheat the oven to 180°C (350°F), Gas mark 4. Put the butter, golden syrup and sugar in a pan and heat gently until the butter has melted and the sugar dissolved.

④ Remove the mixture from the heat. Stir in the flour, ground ginger and chopped stem ginger. Mix thoroughly. It should form a soft dough that leaves the sides of the pan clean. Put teaspoonfuls of the mixture onto a parchment lined baking sheet, spaced about 2.5 cm (1 in) apart to allow room for the biscuits to spread as they cook. Bake for 10–12 minutes until the biscuits are cooked through and golden brown. Remove from the paper and cool on a wire rack.

⑤ Arrange the mango fools on plates with the stem ginger biscuits to the side to serve.

puddy LOVE

This pudding is also fabulous made with day-old brioche or croissants. If you don't fancy using marmalade try using lemon curd instead.

Bread and butter pudding with marmalade

Serves 6–8

50 g (2 oz) butter, at room temperature plus extra for greasing

1 fruit soda (slightly stale is fine)

5 tbsp marmalade

300 ml (½ pint) cream

300 ml (½ pint) milk

6 egg yolks

75 g (3 oz) golden caster sugar, plus extra to finish

To download the shopping list:
www.superquinn.ie/content/BreadAnd
ButterPuddingWithMarmalade/983

Wine match
Australian Riesling
The sweetness of the Australian Riesling brings out the orange flavours in this dish beautifully.

① Generously butter a 1.75 litre (3 pint) shallow ovenproof dish. Carefully cut away the crusts from the bread and then cut into even-sized slices, then spread with the butter. Spread two-thirds of the slices with four tablespoons of the marmalade. Arrange half of the marmalade bread slices in the bottom of the prepared dish in a slightly overlapping layer. Repeat once more and then finish with the final layer of buttered bread without any marmalade.

② To make the custard, heat the cream and milk in a pan until it almost comes to the boil. Remove from the heat. Meanwhile, whisk together the egg yolks and sugar in a large heatproof bowl set over a pan of simmering water until thickened and the whisk leaves a trail in the mixture. Remove from the heat and beat in the cream mixture until well combined. Pour the warm custard over the layered-up bread slices and leave to stand for 20–30 minutes or until the bread has soaked up most of the custard.

③ Preheat the oven to 180°C (350°F), Gas mark 4 and bake the bread and butter pudding for 25–30 minutes until the custard is just set. Preheat the grill to medium-high. Gently warm the remaining tablespoon of marmalade and brush on top of the cooked bread and butter pudding, then slide under the grill to glaze. Cut into slices and place in wide-rimmed bowls to serve.

Chef's top tip –

If you're looking for a really smooth and creamy finish, try baking in a Bain-marie (that's a roasting tin three-quarters filled with water).

good
HEARTED

Rice pudding is loved by everyone, and it's one of the nations favorite desserts. It's delicious served on its own or with whatever fruit is in season. Strawberries or blueberries especially work well instead of the raspberries.

Old fashioned rice pudding with raspberry compote

Serves 4

100 g (4 oz) pudding rice (short-grain)

600 ml (1 pint) milk

2 tbsp golden caster sugar

1 vanilla pod, cut in half and seeds scraped out

For the raspberry compote:

4 tbsp golden caster sugar

225 g (8 oz) raspberries

To download the shopping list:
www.superquinn.ie/content/OldFashioned
RicePuddingWithRaspberryCompote/984

① To make the rice pudding, place the rice in a deep-sided pan with the milk, sugar and vanilla seeds. Give it all a good stir and then simmer gently for about 30 minutes until the rice pudding is thick and creamy, stirring occasionally.

② Meanwhile, make the raspberry compote. Place the sugar in a pan with the raspberries and using your hands really mush them up so that the raspberry juice releases and dissolves the sugar. Place on the heat and simmer gently for a couple of minutes until slightly thickened but some of the raspberries are just holding their shape.

③ Divide the rice pudding among warmed bowls and add a large spoonful of the raspberry compote to each one to serve.

Wine match
Rutherglen Muscat
The Muscat is the perfect partner for this desert to accentuate the raspberry compote and compliment the creaminess of the rice.

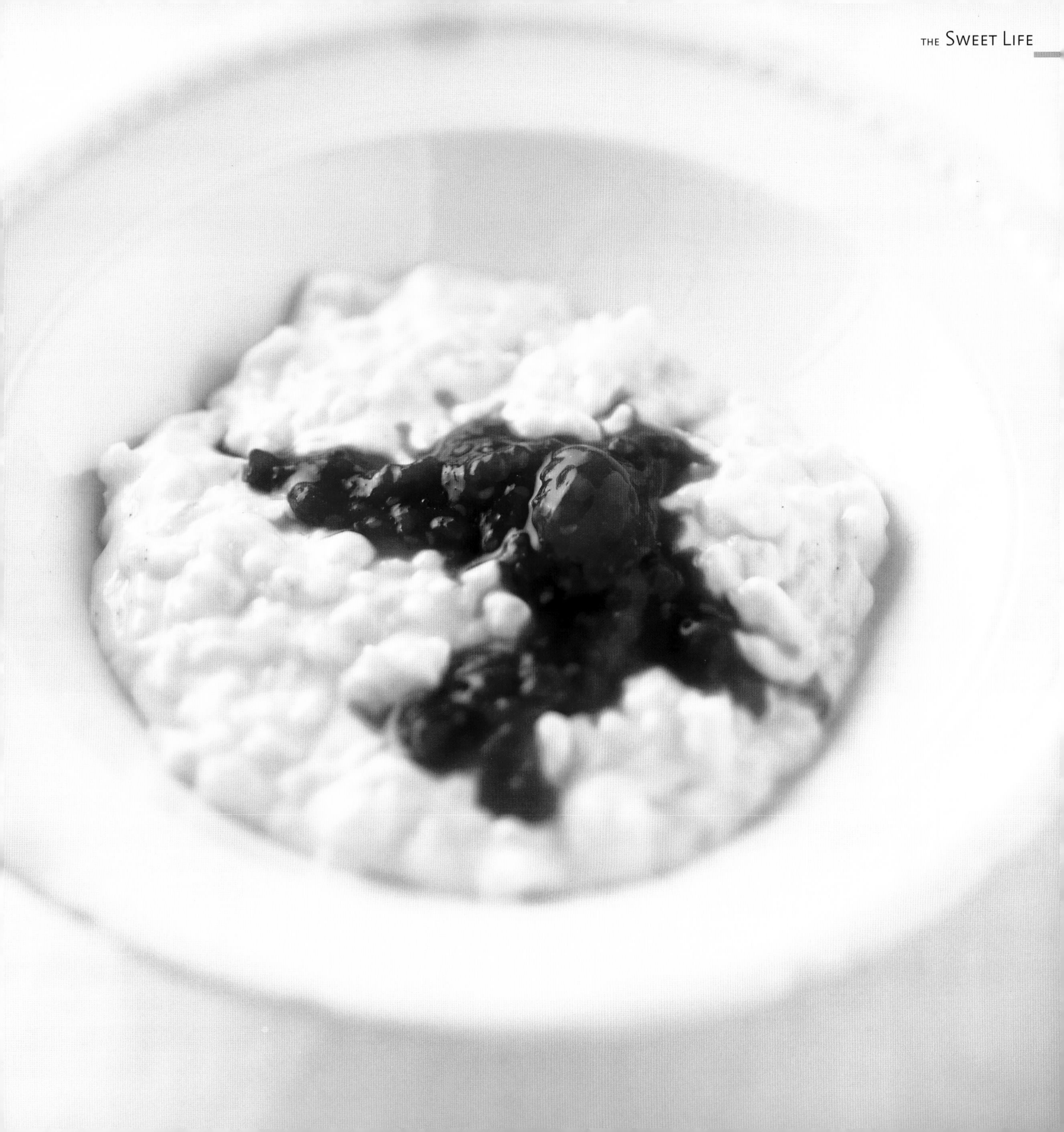

pick and MIX

The elderflower cordial in this crumble gives this dessert a wonderful subtle fragrance. Of course, you could make it with any fruit that is in season, such as apricots, peaches or gooseberries.

Blackberry and elderflower crumble

Serves 4–6

550 g (1 ¼ lb) blackberries

6 tbsp elderflower cordial

175 g (6 oz) plain flour

1 tbsp dried skimmed milk (from a carton)

75 g (3 oz) butter, diced

3 tbsp golden caster sugar

25 g (1 oz) blanched almonds, finely chopped

lightly whipped cream or warm custard, to serve

To download the shopping list:
www.superquinn.ie/content/Blackberry
AndElderflowerCrumble/986

1 Preheat the oven to 200°C (400°F), Gas mark 6. Place the blackberries in an ovenproof dish and sprinkle over the elderflower cordial.

2 Place the flour in a bowl and rub in the butter until the mixture resembles fine breadcrumbs. Stir in the skimmed milk powder, sugar and almonds. Sprinkle the crumble topping over the blackberry mixture and bake for 25–30 minutes or until the crumble topping is golden brown and the blackberry juice is bubbling around the sides. Serve straight to the table and divide among wide-rimmed bowls to serve with some lightly whipped cream or warm custard.

Wine match
Rutherglen Muscat
The subtle flavour of the elderflower and the blackberries calls for a sweet red wine like the Rutherglen Muscat.

Chef's top tip –
The skimmed milk powder gives the crumble a wonderful richness and helps thicken the juices from the blackberries.

CUSTOMER RECIPE — MAURA NOLAN,
SUPERQUINN CARLOW

ROLLout

Chocolate Swiss roll with mixed berries

"This classic Swiss roll is best enjoyed on the day it is made. To make your own raspberry coulis, blitz raspberries with a little icing sugar to sweeten and then pass through a fine sieve. I sometimes mix a couple of tablespoons of framboise liqueur with the coulis for an extra punch."

Serves 6–8

4 eggs

100 g (4 oz) caster sugar, plus extra for dusting

75 g (3 oz) plain flour

25 g (1 oz) cocoa powder

250 ml carton cream

4 tbsp raspberry coulis (from a bottle)

150 g (5 oz) mixed berries, such as raspberries, blueberries and blackberries

To download the shopping list:
www.superquinn.ie/content/Chocolate
SwissRollWithMixedBerries/987

MAURA lives in Carlow and finds that Superquinn is the perfect place to shop as she really enjoys spending time in the kitchen trying new dishes to entertain family and friends.

① Preheat the oven to 200°C (400°F), Gas mark 6. Line a 33 x 23cm (13 x 9 in) Swiss roll tin with parchment paper. Put the eggs and sugar in a large heatproof bowl over a pan of hot water and whisk until the mixture has doubled in volume and is thick enough to leave a trail on the surface when the beaters are lifted. Remove the bowl from the pan and whisk for 5 minutes or until cool.

② Sift the flour and cocoa powder into a separate bowl and then gently tip into the cooled egg mixture. Using a large metal spoon, fold in very gently until just combined. Pour the mixture into the prepared tin, tilting the tin to spread it out in an even layer. Bake for 10–12 minutes until well risen and firm to the touch.

③ Meanwhile, place a sheet of parchment paper on the work surface and dust with caster sugar. Quickly turn the cake onto the paper and trim off the crusty edges and roll up with the paper inside.

④ Whip the cream in a bowl until soft peaks have formed. When the Swiss roll is cold, carefully unroll and spread with the raspberry coulis, leaving a 1 cm (½ in) border around the edges and then cover with the whipped cream. Scatter over the berries and re-roll. Arrange on a platter and serve straight to the table.

Chef's top tip —

Do not be tempted to use a palette knife or spatula to smooth the uncooked mixture into the sides of the tin as this would crush the air bubbles.

Wine match
Sauternes
The sweetness of the Sauternes really lifts the fruitiness of the mixed berries.

I can do
SLICE

This dessert is worth leaving at room temperature for a couple of hours before serving to allow the flavour of the syrup to penetrate the pineapple.

Fanned pineapple with lemongrass and chilli syrup

Serves 6–8

50 g (2 oz) caster sugar

1 lemongrass stick

1 cm (½ in) piece fresh root ginger, peeled

1 large ripe pineapple

1 small mild red chilli, seeded and finely chopped

1 tbsp shredded fresh mint leaves

mango sorbet, to serve

Wine match
Australian Riesling
The tartness of the pineapple is balanced beautifully with the sweetness of the Australian Riesling.

To download the shopping list:
www.superquinn.ie/content/Fanned
PineappleWithLemongrassAndChilliSyrup/985

1 Put the sugar into a pan with four tablespoons of water. Bring to a simmer, stirring until the sugar has completely dissolved. Trim down the lemongrass and then bash it with the back of a large knife to help release all its flavour. Cut the ginger into slices and add to the sugar syrup with the lemongrass. Cook for 1–2 minutes. Remove the pan from the heat and set aside to infuse until the mixture is completely cold. Then remove and discard the pieces of lemongrass and ginger. Stir in the chilli and mint.

2 Slice the top and bottom off the pineapple, sit it upright on a board and slice away the skin and all the little brown bits. Cut into quarters and then using a Japanese mandolin or very sharp knife, slice the pineapple as thinly as possible. Cut out the cores, which can be quite woody. Arrange on plates in a thin slightly overlapping layer. If time allows, leave at room temperature for a couple of hours covered with cling film before serving with scoops of the mango sorbet.

INDEX
by course

Starters & Sides

Salads

Snacks

Mains

Desserts

Breads, Cakes & Cookies

alphabetcial INDEX